RESULTS

The Key to Continuous School Improvement

2nd Edition

MIKE SCHMOKER

Association for Supervision and Curriculum Development
Alexandria, Virginia USA

Association for Supervision and Curriculum Development
1703 N. Beauregard St. • Alexandria, VA 22311-1714 USA
Telephone: 1-800-933-2723 or 703-578-9600 • Fax: 703-575-5400
Web site: http://www.ascd.org • E-mail: member@ascd.org

Gene R. Carter, *Executive Director*
Michelle Terry, *Associate Executive Director, Program Development*
Nancy Modrak, *Director, Publishing*
John O'Neil, *Director of Acquisitions*
Julie Houtz, *Managing Editor of Books*
Carolyn R. Pool, *Associate Editor*
Charles D. Halverson, *Project Assistant*
Gary Bloom, *Director, Design and Production Services*
Karen Monaco, *Senior Designer*
Tracey A. Smith, *Production Manager*
Dina Murray, *Production Coordinator*
John Franklin, *Production Coordinator*
Valerie Sprague, *Desktop Publisher*
Winfield Swanson, *Indexer*

Printed in the United States of America.

s8/1999

ASCD Stock No. 199233
ASCD member price: $16.95   nonmember price: $20.95

Library of Congress Cataloging-in-Publication Data
Schmoker, Michael J.
  Results : the key to continuous school improvement / Mike Schmoker. — 2nd ed.
    p. cm.
  Includes bibliographical references (p.) and index.
  ISBN 0-87120-356-1 (alk. paper)
    1. School improvement programs—United States. 2. Educational change—United States. 3. Education—Aims and objectives—United States. I. Title. II. Title: Key to continuous school improvement
  LB2822.82 .S35 1999
  371.2'00973—dc21   99-37231
                                                          CIP

04 03 02 01   10 9 8 7 6 5 4

*For James Bartell and Richard Wood,
teachers who made all the difference,
and for
Ron Brandt and Don Scott,
who encouraged me.*

The problem is not tests per se but the failure…to be results focused and data driven. Coaches regularly adjust performance in light of ongoing results, even dramatically altering their lesson plans in light of unexpectedly poor results.

—Grant Wiggins

We can, whenever and wherever we choose, successfully teach all children whose schooling is of interest to us.

—Ron Edmonds

Results: The Key to Continuous School Improvement

2nd edition

Foreword *by Michael Fullan*		vii
Preface to 2nd Edition		ix
Introduction		1
1	Effective Teamwork	9
2	Measurable Goals	22
3	Performance Data	35
4	Rapid Results: The Breakthrough Strategy	56
5	Research and Development	70
6	Redefining Results	77
7	Opportunities for Action Within and Among the Subject Areas	89
Conclusion: Leadership		111
Appendix		119
References		121
Index		129
About the Author		136

Foreword

By Michael Fullan

With all the overload, fragmentation, and profound confusion about the meaning of educational reform and improvement, it is great to see a book that actually contributes to coherence and clarity on the topic. At the same time, it gives us practical ideas and reasons for optimism about getting results in student learning. This second edition of *Results* is a book that tells us, shows us, urges us to use what we know to make a difference in the learning lives of students.

Much of this knowledge is recent, and Mike Schmoker captures the leading edge of the field in laying out what we need to know and be able to do to improve our schools. In recent publications, I concluded that the main problem with educational systems and corresponding innovation and policy making is that they are intrinsically, endemically, inevitably *overloaded and fragmented* (Fullan 1999). Therefore, the main solutions have to be ones that contribute to "coherence making" and "connectedness." One of those solutions is what we call *assessment literacy* (Hargreaves & Fullan 1998). Assessment literacy is

1. The capacity of teachers (individually, but especially together) to examine student achievement data and student work, and make critical sense of it;

2. The more difficult capacity of developing and implementing classroom and school improvement plans arising from the data and designed to get better results; and

3. The political "capacity" to enter the debate and to be positively influential in discussions about the uses and misuses of achievement data.

Schmoker gives us the ammunition to become "assessment literate." The conceptual framework is there—teamwork, goals, performance data, accelerating results, drawing on the knowledge base— as is the need to act through broad-based leadership.

Schmoker provides countless, real examples of *named* schools and districts that took action based on the core principles and then got results—many of them in remarkably short periods.

Outcomes-based education and assessment accountability are finally beginning to come of age, but in a fundamentally redefined format. Results for learning is a "coherence-making strategy." This book gives us the rationale, the framework, and plentiful practical examples of redefining educational reform as not which schools can be most innovative, but rather which schools can be most purposeful. The key, as Schmoker says, is to "redefine" results, both in terms of content (i.e., broaden the definition of *what counts as learning*) and in terms of process (how to use results as a data-driven strategy for reform). Schmoker makes major contributions to both content and process in helping us to maximize the impact of using results to promote continuous school improvement.

The second edition of *Results: The Key to Continuous School Improvement* is a powerful new book in a new field that has enormous importance for making a difference in the future lives of students.

References

Fullan, M. (1999). *Change Forces: The Sequel*. Philadelphia: Falmer Press.

Hargreaves, A., & M. Fullan. (1998). *What's Worth Fighting For Out There?* New York: Teachers College Press; Toronto: Elementary Teachers' Federation of Ontario.

Michael Fullan is Dean, Ontario Institute for Studies in Education, University of Toronto, 252 Bloor St. W, 12-130, Toronto, ON M5S 1V6 (e-mail: mfullan@oise.utoronto.ca).

Preface to the 2nd Edition

The success of the 1st edition of *Results* has been very gratifying. I believe its success is largely owed to those whose real-life success stories fill its pages.

Since its publication, the combined efforts of innumerable people have resulted in great progress on the school improvement front. It is far easier to talk to audiences of educators about using data—sensibly—for improvement purposes. Educators seem much more apt to take a critical, professional view of initiatives and the evidence base that supports—or doesn't support—their use. And more schools than ever are rejecting vague, multiple "improvement goals" in favor of clear, measurable achievement goals. This is perhaps the best development of all. The recent NAEP data—showing record levels of achievement at elementary, middle, and high school levels—speak to this.

For my part, in this 2nd edition of *Results,* I have tried to address those areas where I think improvement is still needed. I have included new material and a number of new examples that I hope will more clearly illustrate the power of focusing on certain essential elements of improvement.

I have included significant new material in the area of teamwork—an area where others have asked me to be more explicit. Chiefly, we need to be more disciplined and systematic in our professional collaboration—and to be single-minded in our concern with *identifying and then solving particularly difficult instructional and learning problems.* No proven program or strategy will ever replace the need for focused collaboration and applied intelligence at the ground level. We must cultivate a new professional ethos, not unlike what obtains in places like Silicon Valley—of everyone at all times inventing, adapting, refining, adding to, disseminating, and then recognizing and rewarding new and more effective practices that get results. I have also included a section on the need for such focused, structured, goal-oriented collaboration at the administrative level, as well.

I've tried to clarify and define improvement goals and subgoals with an emphasis on even greater simplicity and economy. The implications of the Third International Math and Science Study (TIMSS)—that less *really is* more—is full of both hope and challenge;

perhaps our most persistent and unfortunate habit is our tendency to complicate and overload our systems and the people in them.

Chapter 5, on research-based practices, has been beefed up to include more strategies and cases of their successful use. It is only too apparent that our knowledge base is still vastly underused and yet brimming with potential both for improved results and for transforming the teaching profession. The recent legislation that funds research-based comprehensive reform programs is a heartening development. The disturbing thing is that the evidence base for many of these so-called research-based programs is surprisingly weak. Such comprehensive but less effective programs divert us from the better research on simple, usable instructional strategies that are still ignored in the majority of classrooms. It is time for teams of practitioners to tap into the power of best practice while continuously engaging in results-oriented "action research." We have learned a great deal, but the task for us now is to creatively and systematically add to and adapt the best we know.

Throughout, I have also added material on the power and necessity of teacher leadership; of effective annual and ongoing assessment; and of the importance of a more strict and deliberate "alignment" among key elements like improvement goals, staff development, teamwork, instruction, and assessment. The last chapter provides additional examples and suggestions for capitalizing on the still underappreciated power of reward, recognition, and celebration structures in the life of schools that are serious about improving.

Finally, I would like to thank the many people in schools I have visited whose work and results have added so much to my learning. I would also like to thank people like Linda Darling-Hammond, Rick DuFour, Michael Fullan, Stephanie Hirsh, Bob Marzano, Lynda Peddy, Jan Rowe, Dennis Sparks, Grant Wiggins, and Harry Wong. Their work and words, written and spoken, have inspired me and contributed inestimably to my work. They have added to my sense of hope and optimism that we can succeed in this ambitious venture to truly educate record numbers of students.

MIKE SCHMOKER
Englewood, Colorado
July 1999

Introduction

Schools, classrooms, and school systems can and do improve, and the factors facilitating improvement are neither so exotic, unusual, or expensive that they are beyond the grasp of...ordinary schools.

—Clark, Lotto, and Astuto 1984

The annual goal statements that emerge from school improvement efforts are rarely linked to student achievement, and they seldom challenge the basic elements of practice.

—McGonagill 1992

School improvement is not a mystery. Incremental, even dramatic, improvement is not only possible but probable under the right conditions. The purpose of this book is to elaborate on the simple conditions that favor results, briefly discuss the theory behind the conditions, and demonstrate, using examples from schools, how anyone in virtually any school setting can begin to successfully replicate these conditions.

A recurrent theme is an emphasis on principles and practices that (1) are simple and supported by research, (2) are relatively few in number, and (3) have huge but underused potential. Consider only this—school goals are "rarely linked to student achievement" (McGonagill 1992). We don't need to look any further for why the school improvement movement, for all the knowledge it has generated and passion it has aroused, is moving forward at such a relatively slow pace. Perhaps this is a function of what Fullan and Miles (1992) write in an examination of school reform:

> Reform often fails because politics often favors symbols over substance. Substantial change in practice requires a lot of hard and clever work "on the ground," which is not the strong point of political players (p. 746).

Our concern with politics has caused us to overlook the most obvious on-the-ground concerns about our real purposes—our goals.

1

We have launched initiatives (e.g., site-based management), provided loads of staff development in certain methods (e.g., "Essential Elements of Instruction"), and spent untold hours drawing up visions and mission statements. All had promise. But these symbolic, high-profile "initiatives du jour" occurred in the near absence of any written or explicit intention to monitor, adjust, and thus palpably increase student learning or achievement. The combination of three concepts constitutes the foundation for results: meaningful, informed teamwork; clear, measurable goals; and the regular collection and analysis of performance data. Chapters 1–3 describe these results and explore these three concepts, which have a remarkable potential for transforming almost any school or district.

In this era of heightened interest in school reform, we have yet to realize that organizations typically get what they earnestly and specifically set out to get. Good-faith efforts to establish goals and then to collectively and regularly monitor and adjust actions toward them produce results.

We have to acknowledge that people work more effectively, efficiently, and persistently when they work collectively, while gauging their efforts against results (Rosenholtz 1991). Results goad, guide, and motivate groups and individuals. Experience by itself does not adequately inform us of the quality of education we are providing. It typically thwarts innovation (Little 1990), tending to encourage teachers and administrators to carry out activities as they always have, regardless of whether an activity's effectiveness can be demonstrated.

Twenty-six years ago, John Goodlad (Goodlad, Klein, and Associates 1970) told us that even "innovation" is not enough, that "behind the classroom door," even teachers who think they are implementing an innovation are often only "twisting" it right back into what they have always done (p. 72). We have been naive; without the reference point that results provide, experience is often a slow and misleading teacher. Informed changes in practice can produce timely, even rapid, incremental advances. There are ways to promote such steady and rapid improvement. They are the subject of Chapter 4.

Overreliance on first-person experience prevents improvement and keeps educators from seeking other information sources, such as effective, formal research on best practices or their consequences (Little 1990). This is unfortunate, considering the rich legacy of what we have learned in the last 30 years about how to improve schools, districts, and classroom instruction. We have not come close to taking advantage of this knowledge. I explore this issue throughout the book, especially in Chapter 5.

My aim is to spotlight a handful of essential concepts that others have developed but that perhaps have not received sufficient attention where they matter most—in classrooms and schools. Much of the best that we know has been lost in the mass of information and issues that have competed for the spotlight over the years. In this chaos, we remembered "reform" and "restructuring" in all their bewildering manifestations. But we may have inadvertently over-looked what is both the cause and effect of school improvement—concrete improvement itself. The principles and schools that are cited here can provide a good beginning. If we wish to move more effectively from means to ends, we must do a better job of "connecting the dots."

Education literature contains numerous references to results. But results have rarely become operational. And, as I try to show, schools have an almost cultural and ingrained aversion to reckoning with, much less living by, results. A deep and debilitating confusion about how means relate to ends has always been one of the marks of the teaching profession (Lortie 1975, Sizer 1992).

The word "results" may even seem troublesome. It has been dragged in and out of many contexts, sounding sensible one moment, retrograde the next. We are sometimes uneasy about its use: Some reject it for representing an implicit disregard for "process." For others, it carries the unspoken implication that results must be obtained at any cost or at the expense of what is truly best for children.

Concepts that seem to have been borrowed from business are often misunderstood. They are made to bear the burden of every sinister possibility, raising fears of a ruthless and mechanistic perversion of schooling that will supplant the best that schools now do. Looking for results may even smack of the worst kind of accountability: an exclusive insistence on raising test scores.

"Results" does not have such a narrow meaning in this book. Chapters 6 and 7 suggest how we can move beyond a limited view of achievement to one that embraces both standardized testing as well as the exciting recent advances in alternative assessment. Results should be understood as a thoughtfully established, desired end-product, as evidence that something worked (or did not work). In this sense, all results—good or bad—are ultimately good, because they provide feedback that can guide us, telling us *what to do next* and how to do it better. Feedback, then, is synonymous with results. And though results have some connection to accountability, that connection is only one dimension of its importance.

An emphasis on results is central to school improvement. We are seeing that such improvement undeniably affects the lives of children, what they earn, and what they become (Bishop 1995). This effect cannot be taken for granted. We still do not give results the central concern they deserve; thus, we have neglected the actions and attitudes that will help us get better results. We talk as though we want results, but we generally fail to make the kind of systematic, organized effort that produces them. The principles examined are intended to close the gap between intent and successful "on-the-ground" effort toward improvement.

Concentrating on results does not negate the importance of process. On the contrary, the two are interdependent: Results tell us which processes are most effective and *to what extent* and where processes need reexamining and adjusting. Processes exist for results—and results should inform processes. We cannot afford to emphasize one over the other. "We fail," writes Wiggins, to "regularly adjust performance in light of ongoing results" (1994a, p. 18).

Curiously, a virulent reaction against an emphasis on results has occurred in unlikely places. Until recently, some of those involved in the Total Quality Management (TQM) movement were uneasy about such a focus. There are reasons for this concern: Many in business are justifiably wary of what happens when the wrong kinds of results govern us. A frequently cited example is quarterly profits, which can compromise long-term growth and quality.

To avoid this pitfall, educators need to be thoughtful and discriminating, taking the lead in defining—and redefining—results. Teachers need to look at student ability to write effectively, read critically, retain information, perform, present, apply, calculate, and analyze. Schools can evaluate these activities and the processes that inform them immediately, within and increasingly among the disciplines (see Chapters 6 and 7). Thoughtlessly rejecting a focus on results should be resisted. Unfortunately, schools typically have been guilty of shorting both processes and results.

The average school still "puts its faith in process, not in results" (Fiske 1992, p. 116). Kevin Castner, former assistant superintendent of schools in Frederick County, Maryland, refers to our "disease of being accountable only for process and procedures" (Bullard and Taylor 1993, p. 80). Educators need to reconceptualize how processes and results interact and refine processes both before and during implementation. Emphasizing only one major or untested process, without careful and frequent analysis, can be disastrous. An example is when the New York City schools poured $120 million into a single process, guidance services, which had never been tested against results. Four years later, the district found that the process did not affect their goal—to reduce the dropout rate. They later discovered the real problem: They needed to make teaching "more appealing to students" (Fiske 1992, p. 64).

Similarly, we implement a range of elaborate processes—such as site-based management, cooperative learning, and whole language instruction—without adequately monitoring the impact. These changes are deep. Regular monitoring, followed by adjustment, is the only way to expect success. History has demonstrated that translating theory into practice, though important, is not enough. We also need an ongoing concern with the real impact we are having. Otherwise, after all our training and fanfare, even the most promising innovations often dissipate into insignificance, as we have seen happen with so many potentially beneficial programs (e.g., the middle school movement, which avoided the use of data for monitoring and improvement purposes. Alas, even its most passionate advocates lament its failure to realize the improvement it was intended to promote [Lounsbury and Clark 1990, Gitlin 1990, Lipsitz and Felner 1997]). As I heard Grant Wiggins say at a recent conference, schools never "pilot" new programs or processes; we just send them off and then "wave at them from the pier, never to be seen again."

A concern with results can remedy this lack without forcing us into the mistakes or excesses of the past. Processes and results are cooperative. The problem is failing to concern ourselves with carefully selected results—and a more precise understanding of which processes most favor them.

Results: The Key to Quality and Improvement

A remarkable finding has emerged about the organizations that succeed: They are concerned with processes only insofar as *these processes affect results* (Brigham 1994). In addition, they are concerned with short-term as well as long-range results. Short-term results act as vital feedback and provide encouragement and momentum toward continued improvement (Schaffer and Thomson 1992).

Employees at the Toyota plant in Georgetown, Kentucky, are concerned with such results as the percentage (measured by tenths of a percentage) of car hoods that fit perfectly in place. In another case, the results of introducing a new conveyor hook into the process were measured by the number of times a part fell off the hook and into a water bath. The plant concentrates on measurable results, such as reliability and repair records, the percentage of cars arriving on the lot in perfect condition, and customer satisfaction data. Processes are always "in the rough"; concern with results ensures that all *processes* are perpetually scrutinized for adjustments. The results at places like Toyota, as well as the schools and organizations this book examines, are intimately connected to processes.

What About Outcomes?

An honest look at schools, districts, and classrooms shows a tenuous relationship between processes and results. This is particularly unfortunate in the wake of what was known as the outcome-based movement, the ostensible intent of which was to bring educational results into sharper focus, to finally shed an absorption with inputs in favor of, well, results. The movement did not turn out that way. Why? Because, for all the good that this movement has done in helping us examine and define educational outcomes, it subtly lost its concern with continuous, information-based improvement. Among so-called outcome-based schools and districts, one could rarely find any systematic means to analyze outputs against instruction and inputs. An *Educational Leadership* article reveals that despite all the time, talk, and conferences attended, only a handful of districts showed any real educational benefits from the outcome-based movement. Johnson City schools—clearly a results-oriented district—come to mind. But they are the exception. Research documenting the effects of outcome-based teaching is rare: "Testimonials, speeches, and narrative descriptions may be inspirational and helpful, but they provide little solid ground on which to build a reform movement" (Evans and King 1994, p. 12). This movement was heralded as "the greatest reform of all," because it would put an end to our addiction to change for change's sake.

The recent ferment about outcome-based education (OBE) does not erase the fact that we all *want better outcomes*. The best aspects of the outcome-based movement had—and still have—an excellent chance of bringing us around to the business of striving for and getting better results. That it did not should alert us to a tendency in schools to avert the confrontation that is at the heart of a true results orientation.

Time for a Breakthrough

We have avoided the difficult though promising task of analyzing what we are doing against the results we are getting. We have learned much about assessment, criteria, and rubrics; brain theory; and ways to make learning more active and engaging. Educational research has given us what systems theorist Peter Senge considers to be the most profound set of discoveries in U.S. history. With all this knowledge, we are dancing on the edge of a revolution in the quality of education we can provide, and arguably, our quality of life. Yet, most schools still do not (1) conscientiously examine the number of students who can do such activities as problem-solve, analyze, calculate, and compose and then (2) adjust instruction and programs accordingly.

Educators can benefit substantially from emphasizing both short-term and long-term results. Incremental, measurable improvement not only can but must occur quickly. But this does not exclude the need for careful and patient planning to bring about systemwide change. Long-term, system-transforming change relies on "immediate successes," which are "essential if people are to increase their confidence and expand their vision of what is possible" (Schaffer 1988, p. 60). Success breeds success; Schaffer calls this the "breakthrough strategy" (see Chapter 4). It accounts for the difference between vision that is realized and vision that only exists on paper. As many have discovered, this strategy explains the success of most successful continuous improvement efforts in industry. We educators ignore this principle at great cost.

Properly understood, a concern with results can promote balanced and sensible action that produces higher achievement on a wide range of assessments. I hope to demonstrate this in the following pages. The following assumptions are the basis for my discussion:

• Though a thorough, long-term, cultural transformation should always be the goal of all reform efforts, it must rely on short-term, measurable successes. These successes will result in cultural change and embody change's most important feature—a radical reorientation toward results.

• We are not operating near our potential. Evidence that schools are grossly underperforming organizations surrounds us. Part of the problem is that schools are not true "organizations" (Donahoe 1993).

• Teachers, like other professionals, perform more effectively—even exponentially so—if they collaborate. Although true, effective collaboration represents a significant change in how most teachers work, it should become an expectation.

• Evidence shows that schools can and will improve if they gear up to strive for increasingly better results by examining and refining the processes that most directly contribute to designated results.

The Highest Stakes

Education has a significant and enduring effect on the students and children who populate our urban, rural, and suburban schools. Preschool programs, good schools, and even "raw" (i.e., excluding other factors) years of education make real differences in people's lives and correlate strongly to the future success of our children and to prosocial, community-building adult behavior—to "changed lives," even among low socioeconomic populations (Berrueta-Clement 1984, Reich 1992). In cognitive areas, effective schools have been found to be more important than background—as much as 6 times more important in reading; 10 times in math (Mortimore and Sammons 1987). A report on education and the economy indicates that "educational attainment is the single most important determinant of a person's success in the labor market.... In the 50 years it has been tracked, the payoff to schooling has never been higher" (Bishop 1995, p. 21). Projections are that demand for the well educated—in number and proportion—will increase and that student payoff will escalate as we enter the 21st century (Bishop 1995).

Can we rise to the occasion? We have already begun. Consider the following results:

- In 1982, none of the students at New York City's Key School could pass the New York City proficiency test in writing. The teachers took deliberate steps to improve students' writing. The following year, 80 percent passed (Hodges 1987).
- The Texas Scholars Program set out to increase the proportion of students taking challenging high school courses. They brought in business professionals to speak at assemblies and to emphasize the workplace importance of succeeding in higher math, chemistry, and physics. Enrollment in these courses doubled and tripled in many cases (Folzenlogen 1993).
- In 1994, an inner-city high school in Poughkeepsie, New York, reached its ultimate goal: to make sure every student attended college. As a result, all 160 of its graduating seniors are headed for college (*Arizona Daily Star* 1994).

Even the best can get better. In 1996, staff at Cherry Creek Schools—a prestigious, high-achieving district near Denver, Colorado—took a hard look at their reading achievement data. They had mean scores in reading that they could be proud of. But they were disturbed to find that only 69 percent of their 1st grade students were reading at grade level. They set improvement goals, and by 1998— only two years later—the percentage was up to 82 percent.

We cannot dismiss the impact of these triumphs on human lives, on real children. The ultimate result of such efforts is the life- and community-transforming power that an excellent education bestows on students. We cannot afford to overlook the rich opportunity that schools have to make a difference.

As the many schools described in this book demonstrate, there is every reason to believe that we can begin providing a better education for all students, of every class, starting now. We can do it by focusing, unwaveringly, on better results and the conditions that promote them.

1

Effective Teamwork

The best thing to invest in right now is collegiality. The number one skill that teachers will need is to be team-based, collegial, sharing their knowledge and wisdom.

—Alan November 1998 (p. 6)

Teams get results.

—Katzenbach and Smith 1993

In Chapters 1–3, I examine the key components that favor results and improvement: teamwork, goals, and the selective and judicious use of data. Individually, they have limited impact; combined, they constitute a powerful force for improvement—without necessarily consuming large amounts of time or money (though, if properly spent, more of each is always desired). Together, these elements cannot help but promote better results in any context, as the many school examples in these pages will affirm.

Success depends on the interdependency between collaboration and goals; between both of these and purpose. Though teamwork is fundamental in this scheme, it is "the means, not the end" (Katzenbach and Smith 1993, p. 12). Similarly, Huberman says that collegiality is not a "legitimate end in itself unless it can be shown to affect...the nature or degree of pupil development" (Huberman, in Fullan 1991, p. 136). Chapter 1 defines and discusses the importance and interdependence of effective team collaboration, goals, and data, essential yet often misunderstood issues.

Teacher Isolation

When Thomas Edison was asked why he was so prolific an inventor, he replied that it was a result of what he called the "multiplier effect." He placed his team of inventors near each other to encourage them to consult with one another so that each member of the team benefitted from the collective intelligence of the group. His teams not only worked better but faster (Smith 1985).

9

We must acknowledge that schools would perform better if teachers worked in focused, supportive teams:

> Collegiality among teachers, as measured by the frequency of communication, mutual support, help, etc., was a strong indicator of implementation success. Virtually every research study on the topic has found this to be the case (Fullan 1991, p. 132).

Unfortunately, teacher isolation—the opposite of teamwork—is one of the most obvious realities of a teacher's life (Lortie 1975). Lortie saw the negative effects of this isolation: "Teacher individualism is not cocky and self-assured; it is hesitant and uneasy" (p. 210). Such isolation promotes professional insecurity. Many teachers, comfortable in their isolation, may find the transition to teamwork a little daunting. But the teachers Lortie (1975) interviewed were wise enough to know that the limited, hermetically sealed world of the classrooms they inhabited did not favor their growth or a sense of confidence that they were doing a job well. Why? Because, as he discovered,

> Individualism combines with presentism to retard the search for occupational knowledge. Teachers who work in isolation cannot create an empirically grounded, semantically potent common language. Unless they develop terms to indicate specific events, discussion will lack the clarity it needs to enlighten practice....Individualism supports presentism by inhibiting work with others in a search for common solutions. Teachers do not undertake the collegial effort which has played so crucial a role in other occupations (p. 212).

This passage is worth rereading. The first point it makes is that teachers, the front line in the battle for school improvement, are working in isolated environments that cut the lifeline of useful information. Such isolation thwarts them in developing common solutions through dialogue. Isolation tacitly assumes that practitioners have nothing to learn from each other. When I look back on when I taught English, nothing is more apparent to me than the fact that isolated experience, by itself, was not the best teacher. And I had virtually no opportunity to learn from my colleagues. We did come together for periodic department meetings, but that type of gathering is not what is meant here by collaboration or teamwork.

The crush of what Lortie calls "presentism"—of myriad daily events and duties—kept us from reflecting collaboratively on such obvious and challenging concerns as how to teach composition more effectively, how to conduct discussions about literature more effectively, and how to make literature exciting. We did not know if or how anyone was teaching composition—or even what that meant. So we worked, consciously or unconsciously, toward our own goals, within the limitations of what each of us knew and did not know. Day-to-day concerns kept us from reflecting on what our most important goals should be.

The absence of a common focus and, by extension, common solutions, can be explained by the absence of what Goodlad (Goodlad et al. 1970) calls clear-cut, specific goals for school at all levels of responsibility. These kinds of goals can only be obtained when professionals regularly collaborate and communicate in an effort to define and reach such goals.

An irrational and indefensible isolation continues to prevent professionals from learning from each other. The bottom line is what kids continue to miss out on as a result.

Isolation is unique to the teaching profession and, by implication, to the whole educational system (Lortie 1975). This observation should shock us, as it did Donald Peterson (1991), former president of Ford Motor Company; Peterson was dismayed by the isolation in which teachers work. A number of circumstances account for this situation: "the organization of space, time, and task seriously constrains interactions" (Little 1990, p. 514); and "the traditional school organization minimizes collective, collegial behavior" (Donahoe 1993, p. 299). School systems in other countries do a far better job of creating regular opportunities for productive planning and interaction (Stevenson 1998).

Because so much inhibits work-related teacher interaction, we might be persuaded to believe that this problem is insurmountable. Not so, as the teacher teams highlighted in this book demonstrate. Everyone in the educational community must work diligently to change the structures that impede teamwork. But meanwhile, we must take advantage of the opportunities that already present themselves—and which others have demonstrated can eventuate in better results.

Benefits

Teachers at Donaldson Elementary School in Tucson, Arizona, were reluctant to spend large chunks of their early-out times in meetings supposedly intended to promote "continuous improvement." But when they began to see collective progress, a direct result of their focused collaboration, the meetings became more meaningful. A good example is what happened when we discussed a key weakness in 2nd grade writing: students' difficulty in writing descriptive settings. After the team brainstormed, a team member proposed having students first draw then describe in writing the setting they imagined for their stories. The number of students able to write high-quality descriptions went from just a few to almost the entire 2nd grade class.

Evidence for the benefits of collaboration, rightly conducted, are overwhelming. The nature of the complex work of teaching "cannot be accomplished by even the most knowledgeable individuals working alone" (Little 1990, p. 520). In the typical school, however, teacher practice is "limited to the boundaries of their own experience," without any outside scrutiny or objective analysis. Such boundaries introduce a "conservative bias," which is the enemy of risk and innovation and a recipe for perpetuating the status quo at a time when change is manifestly necessary (Little 1990, pp. 526–527). Little found a strong relationship between the right kind of collegiality and improvements for both teachers and students:

- Remarkable gains in achievement.
- Higher-quality solutions to problems.
- Increased confidence among all school community members.
- Teachers' ability to support one another's strengths and to accommodate weaknesses.
- The ability to examine and test new ideas, methods, and materials.
- More systematic assistance to beginning teachers.
- An expanded pool of ideas, materials, and methods.

Little also quotes Lortie to make the point that the prevailing isolation in which teachers work does little to "add to the intellectual capital of the profession" (Lortie, in Little 1987, pp. 501–502). In the business of teaching and school improvement, intellectual capital— ideas, fresh solutions, and effective teaching methods—is the most precious commodity.

Business literature from theorists such as Tom Peters and W. Edwards Deming is equally as emphatic about how teamwork benefits intellectual and professional capital. For Deming, "there is no substitute for teamwork"; without it, "dissipation of knowledge and effort, results far from optimum," exists (1986, p. 19).

An excellent resource for this topic is *The Wisdom of Teams* (1993) by Jon Katzenbach and Douglas Smith. Their study of teams in 47 organizations corroborates educational studies by educators like Judith Little and Michael Huberman. "It is obvious that teams outperform individuals," that "learning not only occurs in teams but endures" (Katzenbach and Smith 1993, p. 5). Teams "bring together complementary skills and experiences that, by definition, exceed those of any individual on the team...bringing multiple capabilities to bear on difficult issues" (Katzenbach and Smith 1993, pp. 18–19).

Both author Michael Fullan (private communication 1998) and Dennis Sparks, Executive Director of the National Staff Development Council, have recently remarked that effective collaboration is perhaps the most effective form of staff development. For Sparks,

> The image of the future would be a group of teachers sitting around a table talking about their student's work, learning and asking, "What do we need to do differently to get the work we would like from the kids?" (1998b, p. 19)

We must not undervalue research or the best kind of staff training (the subject of Chapter 5). Nonetheless, as Fullan and Hargreaves (1996) point out, we often underestimate teacher expertise—which emerges in the right kind of focused, targeted teamwork. They exhort us to "avoid creating a culture of dependency among teachers by overrating the expertise of published research and underrating the practical knowledge of teachers" (p. 24). We need more—lots more—of both research and optimistic, instructionally-focused collaboration. Teachers—this may surprise us—learn best from each other (Rosenholtz 1991). The best research on teaching is grossly underused. But it is often the logistical and practical knowledge of teachers that makes or breaks the successful implementation of a research-based strategy or program. And we have all seen improvements occur without the help of published research.

Two 1st grade teachers at Prince Elementary School in Tucson, Arizona, have been getting exceptional results for years with students from one of its least advantaged areas, many of whom arrive with very limited skills. What they have learned from each other has enabled them to ensure that an exceptional percentage of their students leaves 1st grade able to read and write on grade level.

Thunderbolt Middle School in Lake Havasu City, Arizona, adopted the highly effective, research-based "Accelerated Reader" program. But no program is context-proof. The two Title I teachers at this school met regularly to review data on progress and to brainstorm for solutions to time and logistical problems—which will always be with us. As a result of this dialogue, the program—and the results—improved significantly.

At Wilkerson Middle School in Birmingham, Alabama, teacher teamwork was the key to immediate, dramatic improvements in every category and at every grade level. Their home-grown strategies and programs led to a 26-percent increase in reading; schoolwide math gains included a 46-percent improvement in the 6th grade (Cox 1994).

In the area of reading improvement, a tremendous opportunity may await us. I am always impressed with what happens when teachers meet to honestly scrutinize and improve their early elementary reading program after carefully reviewing the research on improvement. Teachers from Peck Elementary School in Arvada, Colorado, chose reading as one of their improvement goals. We met one afternoon to (1) review the research on effective reading instruction and then (2) refine instruction, structures, and time allotments to conform to best practice. Fullan is right: Progress is indeed "a social process." The teams worked both within and among the grade levels to share and develop complementary strategies to ensure better results. At every grade level, the teachers helped one another to see opportunities for significant, positive changes that they could not have implemented by themselves.

As Judith Little discovered, the right kind of teamwork leads to a more effective examination and implementation of best practice. Research, by itself, has had less impact than we would like. Let's face it: The solutions to many local, personal, and logistical problems simply aren't spelled out in the research. In Lake Havasu City, teams focused on improved reading performance. This led to a districtwide examination of best practices and programs. This study required us to review our own resources, to collaborate yet further to allocate those resources, and to invent and then adjust structures and new procedures. This combination of best practice and ongoing collaboration led to better results at several schools—most of them coming in the first year. A school with the district's highest poverty rate—72 percent—made particularly dramatic gains at the end of the 1998 school year.

Collaboration works. And it also addresses an essential social dimension of improvement. Successfully implementing innovative procedures "is very much a social process" (Fullan 1991, p. 84). Studies show that people who are members of effective teams "consistently and without prompting emphasized the fun aspects of their work together" (Katzenbach and Smith 1993, p. 19).

I was struck by this same spirit in dozens of workers from the Toyota plant in Kentucky. When I visited them, miles away from their employment, an ex-jockey told me that on Sunday evenings, he "couldn't wait to get with his team to hit the ground running on Monday mornings." Meaningful, purposeful collaboration addresses the social and emotional demands of teaching (Little 1990). And we should not underestimate the social significance of Little's observation that effective collaboration creates that rare arena in which teachers can receive credit and praise for their "knowledge, skill, and judgement" (pp. 18–19). Teamwork provides opportunities to enjoy the social and psychic satisfactions of collective effort.

The Dark Side of Collegiality

In the face of all this evidence, why do we persist in denying these benefits to the profession? The explanation can be found in our failure to be results oriented. Industry is littered with stories about "quality circles" that came and went. Why? Few realized any palpable results, and so they were regarded as a waste of time—the kiss of death for any innovation. Similarly, many teachers find their first attempts at collaboration clumsy and unrewarding. Subsequently, the time they spend in meetings appears to take away from lesson planning and instruction. Predictably, "unproductive" meetings are abandoned (Little 1987, p. 493).

Unproductive, unrewarding meetings—we have all been to them. And because of these experiences, many people simply do not believe that teams perform better than individuals. Katzenbach and Smith (1993) saw how "members waste time in unproductive discussions, which cause more trouble than they are worth...and actually generate more complaints than constructive results" (p. 20). They regard this problem as a lack of discipline and disciplined action, which embodies the essential conditions that favor productive collaboration.

We must clearly distinguish between effective collaboration and the appearance of teamwork. We can begin by stating what teamwork, for the purposes of this book, is not. "The term collegiality has remained conceptually amorphous....Much that passes for collegiality does not add up to much" (Little 1990, p. 509). Similarly, the word *teamwork* "courts imprecision" (Katzenbach and Smith 1993, p. 19). Much of what we call teamwork or collegiality does not favor nor make explicit what *should* be its end: better results for children. The unfortunate reality is that most of what goes on in the name of collegiality is ineffective or counterproductive. "Most alliances among teachers" are not task oriented at all. Instead, they "appear to be informal, voluntary, and distant from the real work in and of the classroom" (Little 1987, p. 507.) This kind of collegiality not only consumes valuable time but can also promote the consequences of isolation that we deplore:

> I argue that the most common configurations of teacher-to-teacher interaction may do more to bolster isolation than to diminish it; the culture that Lortie described as individualistic, present oriented, and conservative is thus not altered but is indeed perpetuated by the most prevalent examples of teacher collaboration and exchange (Little 1990, p. 511).

Alas, the weaker, more common forms of collegiality "serve only to confirm present practice without evaluating its worth." Collegiality may "supply sympathy of the sort that dissuades teachers from the kind of closer analysis of practice that might yield solutions to recurrent problems" and thus accounts for continuing practices that are its ostensible enemy (Little 1990, p. 517). Less formal kinds of collegiality accommodate, even promote, the course of least resistance. This characteristic is part of the "dark side" of collegiality (Fullan 1991, p. 131).

The "bright side" (if you will) is found less frequently. It is rooted in a concern with results, with what Little calls "joint work" that affects gains and classroom performance and involves monitoring student progress and the "thoughtful, explicit examination of practices and their consequences" (Little 1990, p. 519). Huberman writes that collegiality "is not a fully legitimate end in itself, unless it can be shown to affect...the nature or degree of pupil development" (Huberman, in Fullan 1991, p. 136).

The bright side of collegiality can be found at Northview Elementary School in Manhattan, Kansas. Students realized huge gains between 1983 and 1989, when teachers began to collaborate. In reading, 4th and 6th grade scores on district achievement tests rose from 59 to 100 percent, and from 41 to 97 percent, respectively. In math, 4th grade scores rose from 70 to 100 percent; 6th grade scores, from 31 to 97 percent. How? Principal Dan Yunk began to arrange for teams of teachers to meet routinely to analyze scores, identify strengths and weaknesses, and develop ways to effectively address them (Schmoker and Wilson 1993). Something powerful happens when teachers begin to regularly discuss instructional challenges and their solutions.

Collaboration as Action Research

Effective teamwork that leads to results is a discipline—and requires a scientific disposition. The experience of teams I have worked with confirms Little's 1990 findings that collaboration is not often enough characterized by a "thoughtful, explicit examination of practices *and their consequences*" (p. 519, emphasis added). Effective collaboration is really action research—carefully conducted experimentation with new practices and assessment of them.

Listen Before You Leap

To be most effective, teams must resist the impulse to leap prematurely to solutions and actions. Before selecting and elaborating on a potential solution, we should carefully consider (1) its consistency with what we know from pertinent research and (2) our sense of its probable or potential impact on student learning. To take full advantage of the collective expertise of the team, we can listen carefully—and nonjudgmentally—to each other's best ideas (brainstorming is a fast, efficient way to do this both well and quickly). Listening helps to ensure that we select the best of several alternatives. The collective wisdom of the team can then inform the all-important direction the team will take. This kind of thoughtful approach will have a high payoff in student learning.

Provide Follow-Up

Another problem is lack of follow-up, the failure to begin each meeting with a concise discussion of what worked—and didn't. Too many meetings begin *with no reference to commitments made at the last meeting*. A teacher at an elementary school recently informed me that he and his colleagues were "burned out" on brainstorming (a method we were using to generate and select effective reading improvement strategies). His frustration was justifiable. He was tired, he said, of filling chart paper with ideas and that is the end of it—no follow-up on if or how well the ideas had even been implemented or if they had in fact helped students learn.

Careful, methodical follow-up, essential as we know it to be, has not been education's strong suit. But if we want results, a scientific, systematic examination of effort and effects is essential—and one of the most satisfying professional experiences we can have. For all the difficult conditions we face and work under, such an habitual, relentless search for better methods and structures puts the odds of improvement heavily in our favor.

Create Effective Structures

Collaborative teams must carefully design the format for their work (see the Appendix for a suggested format for an effective 30-minute meeting). Participants should arrive knowing that the meeting will open with questions like the following:

• Were you able to successfully implement the strategy we decided to try at the last meeting? (e.g., provide more time for sustained silent reading).

• What was the impact of the strategy on learning and achievement? What evidence or results can you report? (e.g., students read more fluently or performed better on comprehension tests when we provided more silent reading time; student work revealed growth in an identified area of difficulty or weakness).

• What difficulties did you encounter? (e.g., students are selecting books that are too easy or too difficult for sustained reading time).

• How can we overcome these difficulties? (e.g., by developing a system with the librarian that ensures that students select books at appropriate level).

When the group is ready, it can move on to the next most urgent learning problem relative to the measurable goal (e.g., many students are still having difficulty comprehending main ideas from their reading).
Then the group might do the following:

1. Carefully explore a variety of possible alternatives in light of collective deliberation or proven practice—through brainstorming or discussion of a research-based strategy.
2. Carefully select a strategy or solution that they believe has the greatest potential for impact.
3. Commit—as a team—to experimenting with the new strategy and to being ready to report on student impact and implementation at the next meeting.

Successful teams need to have such focused interaction on a fairly regular basis—probably once a month for each student learning goal that we set. Experience has taught us that any less than six strategically scheduled opportunities per year can kill momentum and severely jeopardize the chances of improvement.

Teamwork That Gets Results

Teams in Amphitheater Schools began to brainstorm for solutions to student problems they had identified by using data. A team from Holaway Elementary School met regularly and used data to determine that the greatest area of difficulty in solving multistep math problems was students' ability to write out the steps that led to math solutions. The team then generated possible strategies:

• Provide students with good examples and models of what the writing should look like.
• Ask students to write each step as they complete it, rather than write the entire problem after they have completed the problem.
• Share the writing rubric more explicitly with the students; give them copies.
• Ask students to start their explanation for each step with the phrase, "I did this because."
• Require that students self-assess their work against a specific rubric before they hand in their work.

These ideas were among others that the team generated during only seven minutes of brainstorming (the entire meeting took only about 30 minutes). Implementing these ideas brought the team closer to its improvement goal by the next month. Such activity generates "intellectual capital," and by not tapping into it, we deny teachers and students a precious and essential resource in helping greater numbers of students receive a higher-quality education.

A good example attesting to the power of teamwork, clear goals, and data analysis is Adlai E. Stevenson High School in Lincolnshire, Illinois. Teachers work in department teams that conduct ongoing analyses of performance data. Superintendent Richard DuFour said that each team meets once a month to collaborate. They analyze results at least four times a year, and the times are built into the calendar. Nine times a year, students come to school at 10:30 a.m. to give teachers time to collaborate. Many schools have benefitted from such late-ins and early-outs, which have been incorporated into school schedules across the United States.

At Stevenson High School, what happened when time was provided for results-oriented teamwork? In 1985, before the process was introduced, the school did not rank in the top 50 schools in the 13-state Midwest region. In 1992, when goals were established and collaborative time was instituted:

> The school ranked first in the region, and by 1994, it was among the top 20 schools in the world....Last year, the school established new records in every traditional indicator of student achievement, including grade distributions, failure rates, average ACT scores, average SAT scores, percentage of honor grades on Advanced Placement examinations, and average scores in each of the five areas of the state achievement test (DuFour 1995, p. 35).

Administrative Collaboration

We have been speaking of teacher collaboration—which is of primary importance. But there is a precious shortage of achievement-focused administrative collaboration. It is well documented that as often as administrators meet, they seldom discuss student learning issues; instead, they focus almost exclusively on procedural or political matters (Smith and Andrews 1989). What would happen if administrative teams carved out even 30 minutes, once a month, to more directly share and discuss triumphs and frustrations, to identify problems, and then brainstorm for ideas and solutions for managing academic improvement?

Just imagine the benefits if administrators began to do their own action research on effective ways to promote a culture of effective collaboration and data-driven improvement? Have administrators nothing to learn from each other? Can we afford to assume that they will learn all they need about improvement on their own? If we can't engage in such action research at the district level, how can we expect teachers to engage in it at the grade and site level?

In many school districts, such discussion is long overdue. Administrators and schools and students have everything to learn and much to gain from doing so.

The Need for Hope and Optimism

For all we have said about an intelligent, scientific approach to improvement, there is an element that transcends any method or mechanism or approach. It is the attitude and spirit of the team.

For starters, learning always requires a measure of humility. Fullan and Hargreaves (1996) found that improved schools are marked by a profound if seemingly obvious feature—the belief that they will never stop learning. As we have seen, there is a strong strain of independence in the teaching profession. It is not always easy to admit that there may be a better way to teach something than the way we have always done it.

Unless...

• the team believes strongly in each member's capacity to develop practical solutions to everyday teaching and learning problems;
• there is a belief that regardless of a school's social or economic circumstances, improvement can and will occur, gradually, but inexorably; and
• the team arrives at each meeting anticipating that informed trial and error will inevitably lead to better teaching and hence to higher learning,

...then no mechanism or set of practices will succeed.

To help us maintain this hope, we must celebrate and elevate success. We should regularly read and learn about schools that have overcome great odds. Staff development in practices that have manifestly had an effect on learning must be a regular feature of our school life. This should not be left to chance. *One of the primary roles of the staff development or district office staff should be the collection, dissemination, analysis, and discussion of success stories from within and outside the district.* Through such positive and proactive means, we can fill the air with hope and optimism about the results that are, in fact, within our reach.

*   *   *

Good teamwork among grade-level, department, school, and administrative teams will give us results we once only dreamed of. Chapter 2 defines the most salient feature of good teamwork, or the "serious collaboration," which Little found to be so rare (1987, p. 513). We have already touched on it: the importance of clear, specific performance goals.

2

Measurable Goals

We did not find a single case in the literature where student learning increased but had not been a central goal.

—Joyce, Wolf, and Calhoun 1993

The goal makes the team.

—Mark Rolewski, Principal, Nash Elementary School

Goals give teamwork meaning. Gene Maeroff (1993) writes that "teams are vehicles for increasing efficiency, effectiveness, and motivation." But what motivates and energizes effective teams? According to Maeroff, the answer is (1) "a clear, elevating goal and (2) a results-driven structure," pointing once again to the interdependency between teamwork and tangible improvement (pp. 514–515). Noel Farmer, former superintendent of Frederick County Public Schools in Frederick, Maryland, discusses the importance of goals:

> If you make the goals clear, inviting and doable, attainable, then the goals themselves will drive you, they really drive you. Teachers and principals that buy into it…the doability of it and the clearness of it, they eventually get to the point where they say, "Hey what's happening here? I'm in a whole new ball game." And you see now that people are finding it very rewarding (Farmer, in Bullard and Taylor 1993, p. 123).

Frederick County schools have been very clear about their goals. The school district has gone from the middle of the pack among Maryland school districts to being first or second in every academic category. During a three-year period, Chapter I students went from 2 to 70 percent on grade level. These dramatic improvements occurred in a district known for emphasizing authentic learning activities and assessment. With these results in hand, the district took the unprecedented step of asking the community to raise taxes expressly for raising teachers' salaries. The community honored their request, at least raising the hope that communities appreciate results and will support us when we help students to achieve them.

Goals drive us. Psychologist Mihalyi Csikszentmihalyi (1990) has made one of the most interesting discoveries in recent times about the connection between goals and happiness: Goals are the stuff of motivation, persistence, and well-being. In language that echoes Farmer's thoughts, he discovered that generally what people enjoy most is pursuing a clear, doable goal that they value. This connection accounts for why many people are as happy or happier at work than at leisure. In the absence of goals, entropy and aimlessness rush in.

Unfortunately, most schools do not make the connection between goals, motivation, and improvement. We have what is perhaps the most striking, contradictory, self-defeating characteristic of schooling and our efforts to improve it: the gap between the need—and intent—to improve academic performance in our schools on the one hand, and the conspicuous and virtual absence of clear, concrete academic goals in most school or district planning efforts on the other. Without explicit learning goals, we are simply not set up and organized for improvement, for results. Only such goals will allow us to analyze, monitor, and adjust practice toward improvement.

Goodlad (Goodlad et al. 1970) lamented the absence of key reforms that we might reasonably expect to find in our schools and school systems. One of them, already acknowledged for decades, is the necessity of "clearly discernible...clear-cut specified goals for schooling at all levels of responsibility" (pp. 12–13). We are still waiting. The lack of clear goals may provide the most credible explanation for why we are still only "inching along" in our effort to improve schooling for U.S. children (Maeroff 1994, p. 52), for why the results of more than 15 years of reform have been so disappointing (Astuto, Clark, Read, McGree, de Koven, and Fernandez 1994; Darling-Hammond 1998; U.S. Department of Education 1998). Rosenholtz (1991) wrote that clear, measurable goals are the "center to the mystery of school's success, mediocrity, or failure." The introduction of specific, measurable goals is among the most promising yet underused strategies we can introduce into school improvement efforts.

A Symbiotic Relationship Between Goals and Teamwork

Failure to establish clear goals for schooling may explain why so much apparent collaboration is futile:

> Far too many teams casually accept goals that are neither demanding, precise, realistic, nor actually held in common.... Teamwork alone never makes a team (Katzenbach and Smith 1993, p. 21).

Goals themselves lead not only to success but also to the effectiveness and cohesion of a team. This concept is different from the conventional notion that only the "right" individuals with suitable chemistry can make an effective team or that team spirit must first be cultivated through a series of team-building activities prior to establishing goals. Viktor Frankl (1963) found that the best way to bring a group of quarrelsome boys together was to provide them with a common goal. Katzenbach and Smith (1993) made the same discovery among the dozens of teams they studied. A clear "common purpose and set of related performance goals," not personality or predisposition, promotes effective teamwork (p. 44).

Little's (1990) research corroborates this same principle: The most effective forms of collegiality succeed "quite apart from their personal friendships or dispositions," and instead depend upon "shared responsibility" for a task that individuals acting alone cannot complete (pp. 519–520). Effective collegiality is a function of having a clear task-orientation, which creates "peer pressure to live up to agreements made." Little (1987) provides an example of a team of teachers who meet with "the explicit aims of improving students' academic achievement" (pp. 494–495). We must recognize the connection between the social, spiritual vitality of a team and its single-minded commitment to performance, the most palpable form of which is a common, objective goal. Peters and Waterman acknowledge this connection:

> Nothing is more enticing than the feeling of being needed, which is the magic that produces high expectations. What's more, if it's your peers who have those high expectations of you, then there's all the more incentive to perform well (Peters and Waterman, in Fullan 1991, p. 83).

Goals and the commitment that they generate are the glue that holds teams together:

> A team's purpose and specific performance goals have a symbiotic relationship; each depends on the other to stay relevant and vital. The specific performance goals help a team track progress and hold itself accountable; the broader, even nobler aspirations in a team's purpose supply both meaning and emotional energy (Katzenbach and Smith 1993, p. 55).

The combination of goals and teamwork is essential to performance. These two elements point up the convergence of economic and social, rational, and emotional factors in improvement initiatives.

As Lortie (1975) and Little (1990) observed, this kind of goal-oriented teamwork is rare in schools. Rosenholtz (1991) made a related observation: The existence of common goals in schools was just as rare, and the lack of agreed-upon goals makes schools unique among organizations. She found that there was very little goal consensus—a collective agreement about what to work toward—even though her studies revealed that this element was the heart of what accounted for progress and success.

Rosenholtz (1991) also found a reciprocal relationship between goals and collegiality: Isolation "undermines the development of shared instructional goals" (p. 17). Without clear, common goals, teachers are not able to communicate meaningfully and precisely about how to improve—and about how to determine if they are improving. Clear goals "promote rational planning and action," as well as "clear criteria by which...performance can be evaluated" (p. 13). When clear goals are absent, schools become "nothing more than collections of independent teachers, each marching to the step of a different pedagogical drum" (p. 17).

At Dodge Park Elementary School in Prince George's County, Maryland, the student body was more than 90 percent poor and minority. Achievement was low—at the 44th percentile on the California Achievement Test. The school established an explicit goal: to raise poor and minority achievement. Educators worked together to develop more effective strategies and to raise expectations. Over the next four years, overall achievement went from the 44th to the 99th percentile. Minority students surpassed their Anglo counterparts by 11 points. They outperformed other minority students in the county by 28 points (Murphy 1988).

School success depends upon how effectively we select, define, and measure progress and how well we adjust effort toward goals. School goals tell teachers what should be emphasized instructionally and define for schools and teachers "how they should gauge their performance success" (Rosenholtz 1991, p. 5).

The lack of common goals actually *promotes* isolation from colleagues, which animates a spiral of fear and insecurity as teachers perceive that their problems are unique (Rosenholtz 1989). This idea parallels Lortie's findings that teachers working in isolation are stymied in their desire to seek help from each other. These conditions interact, intensifying each other: Isolation thwarts common direction, which in turn promotes a deeper sense of isolation as teachers grow further and further apart in what they think and do and in how they pursue tacit or expressed goals. Teachers reach a point where they become set in their ways and therefore more reluctant to consider pursuing common improvement goals.

This is the world of schools. They typically lack clear, common direction and communication that promotes people working toward mutually intelligible goals.

But even goals are not enough: Goal-orientation plus dialogue brings teams closer to their goals. Such dialogue helps teams identify and address instructional and classroom factors that have the best chance of making a difference. A middle school in Richmond County, Georgia, had instituted measures to help at-risk students: lower class size, special programs, and counseling. Nothing happened. It was not until teachers began to meet in study groups to help each other implement more effective teaching strategies that results came. In one year, the average student went from making 6 month's progress to making 10 month's progress. The promotion rate increased from 30 to 70 percent. The following year, it increased again—to 95 percent (Joyce, Wolf, and Calhoun 1993).

If we wish to have energized employees who are steadily progressing toward the ultimate, long-term goal of providing a better, richer education for our students, then every member of every school should be working together in teams, not token or merely social teams, but goal-oriented units.

A Goal-Averse Culture

Initially, the middle school in Richmond County, Georgia, illustrated a problem in education: Efforts are often too far removed from what should be education's primary goal—classroom results. This tendency runs deep. In reviewing 20 student action research project proposals, as well as a popular book on action research, I found only one project that expressed an interest in gauging the project's impact *on students;* the rest focused on general observation and qualitative study of teacher behaviors (which are also important). What is interesting is that in all this research, I found an apparent aversion to gauging what may be the most significant and helpful data and progress—that which reflects the goal of student learning. Our aversion to such goals is manifest.

Donahoe (1993) thinks that the free-lance culture of schools is the primary impediment. After working with a host of schools, he concluded that "schools had no organization." He once told an audience that schools were only "convenient locations for a bunch of individual teachers, like independent contractors." The audience not only accepted this rather stark assessment but "agreed rather enthusiastically" with it. Without deliberate intervention, the culture—in this case, the isolated, relatively goal-free ethos of public schools—will almost always prevail (p. 299).

John Goodlad (Goodlad et al. 1970) made the same discovery: A school's culture was one where, despite the school's intention to implement reforms or new curriculum, the conservative tendency almost always won out. The culture of isolation and privacy generally ensured that innovations were not really implemented. Despite a school's official adoption of new programs, the reality behind the classroom door was not innovative. Evidence indicated that only the most partial, superficial implementation was occurring as teachers found ways to twist the innovation right back into what they had always done.

From General to Common, Measurable Goals

Language can mislead. Efforts that are described using words such as "innovation," "goals," or "purpose" can convince us that we are engaged in substantive change when we may not be. Years into what most schools considered to be profound change, Goodlad and his associates saw no substantive evidence of that change.

Even when schools establish goals, the goals tend to be too general. This unfortunate case of "general goals" creates a sense of "false clarity"—the erroneous belief that we understand and know how to work toward achieving the goals (Fullan 1991, pp. 34–35). Conversely, common, specific goals require focused teamwork to develop common approaches to reaching the goals (Katzenbach and Smith 1993). Such activity promotes clarity and intelligibility and facilitates team members' ability to learn from each other's experience.

I believe that specific goals are the most vital ingredient of purpose. Improvement cannot occur without them. It is no coincidence that Deming's first principle is, "Create constancy of purpose" (1986, p. 23). And a look at Mary Walton's books (1986, 1990) on the success of Deming's methods reveals how closely connected this purpose is to specific, unambiguous goals—reducing turnaround time and waste, meeting deadlines, and meeting or exceeding quality standards.

Why is this specificity so crucial? Rosenholtz (1989) found a number of reasons:

- Specific goals convey a message directly to teachers that they are capable of improvement.
- Specific goals provide a basis for rational decision making, for ways to organize and execute their instruction.
- Specific goals enable teachers to gauge their success.
- Specific goals promote professional dialogue.

Clear goals require us to provide feedback about our progress toward them. This feedback, the vital, frequent flow of information, ensures against the "twisting" Goodlad describes. One cannot twist an innovation when teachers share and examine the feedback about the processes that produce results. Such regular feedback is the key to successful implementation:

> Specific performance goals are an integral part of purpose. Transforming broad directives into specific and measurable performance goals is the surest first step for a team trying to shape a common purpose (Katzenbach and Smith 1993, p. 53).

And yet, institutionally, we continue to ignore the need for feedback. We cherish our typically private, imprecise preferences at the expense of clear and collective goal-orientation. We thus forfeit progress.

Goal-Orientation at Centennial Elementary School

Collective, efficacious, accelerated improvement must of necessity be somewhat public, with the potential for reward—and a measure of risk—which this publicity implies. Centennial Elementary School in Evans, Colorado (Andrade and Ryley 1992), shows how teachers resolved this tension. They have been known to exchange high fives at meetings when they reach monthly improvement goals. But they had to wade through the initial discomfort of allowing the entire school to see how each grade level performed relative to the schoolwide goal of improving student writing skills.

Reflective of the school's TQM approach, student performance results are collected, charted, and analyzed at regular monthly meetings. Teachers see student progress, both at grade level and school level, on a 7-point rubric used throughout the district. To reduce risk (of killing the project), teams report *anonymously*; individual teacher accomplishments are not revealed. But each grade-level team does know that as a member of that school they are expected to perform at a high level. This regular, focused interaction, working toward a common goal, ensures that Centennial teachers speak the same language—the key, as we have seen, to teachers being able to help each other.

The result? Prior to instituting the new process, the schools' writing scores were 16th in a 16-school district for two years. The year they began this goal-oriented approach, they went from 16th to 4th. The power of these simple principles cannot be denied.

In contrast to such clear goal-orientation, Carl Glickman's (1993) experience is worth pondering. It reveals the great distance that still separates us from the many ways of establishing specific, measurable goals for schools. Glickman found himself addressing the faculty of an award-winning school. He asked them to name their school's objectives. The faculty's enthusiastic response was, "To integrate technology into the curriculum."

He thought they misunderstood him. He rephrased it. "No," he said, "What I mean is, what are you trying to accomplish for students?"

The principal then responded, with enthusiastic nods from teachers, that their goal was, "To show that our school can move into the 21st century through technology" (p. 48).

Glickman, with a "nagging feeling of disbelief," stopped pressing them. But during the next few weeks, he asked the same question at 20 other schools. Their responses were telling. Here are examples of the goals they had set:

- Implement whole-language instruction in every classroom.
- Use cooperative learning.
- Develop portfolios and performance assessments.
- Assess learning styles.

Glickman, who has helped many schools improve, believes that such goals are "typical of most 'with it' schools." When he asked people at such schools how they would determine progress and achievement, their responses "reaffirmed his gnawing unrest." They replied that they would gauge their success on whether the innovation had been implemented—*rather than by whether students had learned* (1993, p. 49).

The history of education is littered with attempts to ensure that teachers have learned to use certain innovations. What is less certain is the depth of that learning, whether learning was even remotely connected to student growth—the ostensible intent of education and efforts to improve it.

Glickman believes that the "litmus test for a good school is not its innovations but rather the solid, purposeful, enduring *results* it tries to obtain for its students" (1993, p. 50) (emphasis added).

Goals: The Missing Piece in Reform

When specific goals do not exist, one-shot staff development or high-sounding programs often fill the void. Reporting that an entire staff learned a new program or method is easy; easier still is presuming that this new practice or program will benefit students. But the evidence is clear: Most of what goes on in the name of innovation has a limited impact on student learning.

School reform or restructuring—for example, site-based management—has had disappointing results (Malen, Ogawa, and Kranz 1990). We must remind ourselves that like all innovations, such reforms initially arrived carrying the promise of better results. Site-based management's primary selling point was that it would wrest control from tired, self-serving bureaucracies and turn it over to people whose interests would ensure that schools and school systems would produce better student learning results.

What happened? Not much, according to several studies:

• Despite the time and resources devoted to this huge, widely adopted effort, no documented effect on student learning as a result of site-based management exists (Fullan 1993).

• In Kentucky, where site-based councils have been in place for several years, the councils were no better than the old bureaucracies at focusing on learning. Even an advocate for the changes there admits that site councils have yet to understand that the "ultimate purpose of the councils is to advance student learning" (David 1994, p. 711).

• The outgoing superintendent of Dade County schools, a mecca for those wanting to institute site-based management, left there saying that the impact on achievement "was a wash."

• In Chicago, where the much-heralded move to site-based management seemed so full of promise, the result was no result—not on student learning or even on "the teaching-learning process" (Fullan 1993, p. 123).

We have seen the same thing happen to another major reform: Many schools and districts adopted some form of TQM initiative. Examples of real success, even in districts where the effort is well under way, are rare. A review of almost 100 articles reveals the same disturbing tendency to avoid a concern with goals, with striving for measurable results. Only five articles featured an explicit reference to concrete goals or results, either already achieved or anticipated. Only two goals were related to student learning; one was to improve student scores on weekly spelling tests, an innocuous but hardly inspiring focus. The remaining goals dealt with processes and activities, elaborate planning, partnerships, and new arrangements.

If we concentrate our efforts more on measurable goals, then site-based management and Total Quality can thrive. The past 10 years should have taught us that establishing vague process or procedural goals in the absence of clear, concrete learning goals is foolish. Each undergirds the other. Learning goals give meaning to and act as a healthy check on the traditionally untethered tendency for public institutions to be satisfied with processes, regardless of outcomes.

Osborne and Gaebler (1992), the authors of *Reinventing Govern-*

FIGURE 2.1

Criteria for Effective Goals

- Measurable
- Annual: reflecting an increase over the previous year of the percentage of students achieving mastery—usually in a subject area
- Focused, with occasional exceptions, on student achievement
- Linked to a year-end assessment or other standards-based means of determining if students have reached an established level of performance—usually within a subject area
- Written in simple, direct language that can be understood by almost any audience

---

ment: How the Entrepreneurial Spirit Is Transforming the Public Sector, do not believe that schools have a good record of maintaining a strong or sufficient sense of purpose. They think that without the profit motive, schools do not have enough incentive to establish and pursue palpable improvement. Our record of pouring huge amounts of time and resources into processes (e.g., site-based management), without establishing improved student learning as the goal, probably shocks anyone outside the education establishment.

If we had connected learning goals to site-based management 10 years ago, we would no doubt have much to celebrate now. Because we did not, we have added to a legacy of disillusionment. And we have consumed untold amounts of what Glickman says is the "scarcest resource in school renewal"—time (1993, p. 44).

To obtain the results we want, criteria can be helpful when setting school improvement goals. For example, goals must be measurable, focused on student achievement, and linked to effective assessments (see Figure 2.1).

A representative example might be as follows:

> By the end of the ____ academic year, the percentage of students who are (writing, reading, reaching a standard of performance on a summative assessment) will increase from 52 percent to 60 percent.

Even after we learn to write meaningful, measurable goals, some vital issues can still affect our success with them.

Too Many Goals!

Our failure to exercise a strict economy with regard to time may lead to one of the gravest mistakes we can make: taking on more goals than we can manage. Educational and organizational literature is rife with warnings against this tendency:

• Schaffer (1988) warns against the organizational tendency to "set too many goals...covering too many bases" (p. 29).
• Chang, Labovitz, and Rosansky (1992) offer a recommendation: The number of targeted breakthroughs [should be] explicitly limited to safeguard against all organizations' universal tendency to pursue too many objectives at once (p. 112).
• Joyce, Wolf, and Calhoun (1993) insist that we be "parsimonious about the number of initiatives that are on the table at any time" (p. 44).
• Fullan (1991) warns that attempting too many initiatives at one time can result in "massive failure" (p. 71). "Overload" is perhaps the greatest enemy of improvement (Fullan and Hargreaves 1996).
• Hopkins (1994) observes that "successful schools set priorities for development that are few in number" (p. 185).

Because time is arguably a school's most precious and scarce commodity, we cannot afford to waste it on too many goals. Improvement requires time for planning, training, and constructive dialogue. Donahoe (1993) cites schools that schedule improvement sessions at the beginning of the year for each school goal. Adding a goal requires the consent of the entire staff. If a goal is added, one must be removed. Collective times are "concentrated on a limited number of strategies" and "rigorously allocated to specific aspects of the school's agenda" (pp. 304–305).

Joyce and his colleagues (1993) found that successful teams meet regularly to discuss progress toward goals: weekly, monthly, or quarterly. Schools in our district meet four to six times a year. With that number of meetings, teachers cannot meaningfully analyze progress and generate improvement ideas for more than a few initiatives, especially at first. For Joyce, a school may want to delay initiatives until it can "afford" the time and other resources to implement them properly (p. 38). One way we can make effective use of short meetings is seen in the Appendix.

A Caveat

Now a high school or middle school could have a number of different goals—for each respective course or department. And in some cases, an elementary school may decide to have different goals at different levels—for example, two at primary and two at intermediate. The name of the game is to have each employee involved in no more than a limited number of goals that require the kind of regular time commitment, data analysis, and strategy sessions necessary for success.

A school can also establish minor or related targets, which create focus and concerted effort without needing regular meetings to discuss them. Brief references to successful strategies or progress might be tucked into existing faculty meetings. The following are examples of minor targets for which data can be easily gathered. Such data can heighten awareness and opportunities for celebration and create a sense of progress that feeds the major academic or behavioral goals pursued:

• The number of disciplinary incidents per grading period, with comparisons to last year at the same time.
• Grade-point or rubric data for an important task or ability.
• The percentage of work or assignments students complete.
• The number of teachers completing important training.
• The number of books students read.
• The number of teachers involved in mutual observation for professional improvement.

One of the greatest dangers to a successful improvement effort is losing focus, which results from trying to take on more than we have the time and resources to realistically achieve. Schools are under enormous pressure to respond to every concern their constituents raise. Among the hardest decisions a school community must make is to decide democratically which goals reflect the school's highest priorities—and which it must pursue later. Leaders and facilitators must be prepared to help their faculties and communities exercise discipline and take advantage of such useful tools as weighted or rank-order voting.

Conditions That Encourage Measurable Goals

If we want measurable goals to proliferate, we need to create a climate hospitable to them and to the hard-working individuals who can help us reach them. Peter Senge (1990) is right: If we want better results, we need to look beyond the isolated point or moment or result and into the system that affects the impact we can have. And right now, that system is insensitive to the fact that people work best in a climate that creates high expectations but mitigates against personal threat. Even Susan Rosenholtz (1991), for whom *goals* is a mantra, found that people's willingness to learn from each other and to work hard and persistently toward a challenging goal was a function of a workplace that is not "ego-endangering." Rick Stiggins's work shows that using explicit goals may make teachers more vulnerable to criticism:

> To the extent that you are clear and specific about the outcomes that you take on as your instructional responsibility, you open yourself up to the possibility that some of your students may not be able to hit the target after instruction and there will exist concrete, irrefutable assessment evidence of this....In effect, your supervisor may be able to...muster evidence that you did not succeed in doing what you were hired to do—produce achievement results (1994, p. 64).

Without abandoning the importance of high expectations, sustained change must rely on the human factors that account for a sense of satisfaction and improvement. Kevin Castner, former assistant superintendent of schools in Frederick County, Maryland, calls it "organized enthusiasm." As we have seen, measurable learning goals are the key. They tap into a basic sense of accomplishment and improvement that makes life interesting and challenging.

We know more now that we did years ago, when Goodlad (1970) noted the absence of clear, specific learning goals at every level of our school systems. We recognize how crucial goals are to improvement. It is time we got around to making such goals a universal expectation at every level and school.

Performance Data

When people say they work at a good school, what do they mean?

—Glickman 1993

But what does "pretty well" mean? chided Ralph.

—Byham 1992

What gets measured gets done.

—Peters 1987

Data help us to monitor and assess performance. Just as goals are an essential element of success, so data are an essential piece of working toward goals. As with goals, data must be used judiciously and with discretion.

Lortie writes that "the monitoring of effective instruction is the heart of effective instruction" (1975, p. 141). Colorado's Weld County School District 6 applied this concept when teachers decided to systematically raise overall achievement while addressing the obvious disparities between socioeconomic groups. They introduced many interventions, including a system in which students had to demonstrate competency in writing, reading, and mathematics before graduating to the next level. Students had to move up before moving on.

A crucial component of their new effort was collecting data both monthly and quarterly. The system enabled students to know how they are performing, which helps them focus on continually improving. The system also helped teachers:

> [Teachers] can base teaching decisions on solid data rather than on assumptions, and they can make adjustments early on to avoid the downward spiral of remediation (Waters, Burger, and Burger 1995, p. 39).

Does such a system, as some suspect, result in pushing low-achievers down even further (Noddings 1997)? Apparently not. Over-all achievement increased, and the gap between rich and poor closed considerably—even in such higher-order competencies as writing. Figure 3.1 shows what happened in District 6 after educators intro-duced a writing assessment during the 1988–89 school year.

FIGURE 3.1

Writing Assessment Results for Weld County School District 6 in Colorado

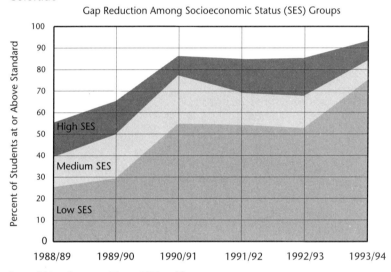

Source: Waters, Burger, and Burger 1995, p. 37.

Data are to goals what signposts are to travelers; data are not end points, but are essential to reaching them—the signposts on the road to school improvement. Thus, data and feedback are interchangeable and should be an essential feature of how schools do business.

The Call for Data

Practitioners frequently say that data do not belong in the educational sphere. Alfie Kohn (1993) takes serious issue with the use of data in schools. He is afraid that emphasizing the measurable will force a shift toward areas that are most easily measured (e.g., spelling tests), or that we will begin to rely on standardized tests and exclude all other measures. Point taken. But we have already seen how teachers are using data to track and improve achievement in writing and higher-order math skills (see Chapter 1). We see other examples in Chapters 6 and 7. Criteria-based assessments and rubrics have changed the nature of assessment by providing numerical data that take us beyond the ability to test mere recall. We can now assess understanding, application, and other thinking skills in new ways.

It is one thing to be circumspect to protect against the abuses or excesses of data; it is something else to flatly reject their use. Are gathering and analyzing data on progress and achievement not needed? Umpteen reforms have come and gone, using up time, money, and hope. They have left a crippling disillusionment in their wake, a cynicism about staff development and any belief that training or innovation benefits students. Not using data to monitor results can be calamitous. Recent examples are those foundations that after spending billions of dollars in grants to innovate, made an interesting discovery: No salient attempt had been made to measure the effects of the innovations (West 1994). Carnine (1993) writes that our current practices for adopting classroom materials and programs, because they do not use achievement data, are at odds with "the results educators and the public are clamoring for" (p. 40). These materials are never classroom tested. He laments the irony of this in light of the 309 billion hours U.S. students spend in schools using such materials.

How long will we continue to avoid using an invaluable tool, capable of telling us how we are doing, what is and is not working, and how to adjust effort toward improvement? Most educators know that we do not adequately monitor student progress. If we did, Grant Wiggins's remark (which I heard him make at a conference in Phoenix, Ariz.) would not invariably get a reaction from audiences:

> Schools don't pilot anything. They just send ideas and inno-
> vations off and wave at them from the pier, never to be seen
> again.

Share this quote with a group of educators; the eruption of knowing laughter says it all. If we look at Deming's "Plan, Do, Study, Act" cycle (1986) (or any of its educational equivalents in the James Comer or Henry Levin schools), we can see that we do, do, do, but seldom study. We fail to examine data that can guide us as we act. No wonder implementation is so often haphazard and why so many innovations do not have the expected impact.

Many enlightened educators recognize that we need data to improve teaching practice:

- In the early 1980s, Ron Edmonds advocated for a more rigorous and frequent concern with performance data when he wrote that "the days are long gone when an educator's best judgement constitutes sufficient proof of learning outcomes." One of the principles of effective schools that he fathered is that successful schools "frequently monitor progress" (Edmonds, in Bullard and Taylor 1993, p. 17).

- For Grant Wiggins, a serious problem facing education is "the failure of classroom teachers...to be results focused and data driven. Coaches regularly adjust performance in light of ongoing results" (1994a, p. 18).

- Matthew Miles tells us that "those steering school improvement need good data on what is happening" (Miles, in Fullan 1991, p. 83).

- Jacqueline and Martin Brooks (1993), in their excellent book about active, constructivist teaching, write that "school-based study groups" must begin "systematically collecting, analyzing, and using these data to inform classroom practices" (p. 125).

- Bruce Joyce and his colleagues (1993), in the name of action research, exhort us to "collect, organize, and interpret on-site data" (p. 8).

- Henry Levin and his associates (Hopfenberg, Levin, Meister, and Roers 1990) call for school improvement that uses "data, on students...qualitative and quantitative information...disaggregated test scores and other measures of student performance" (p. 14).

- Principal Suzanne Still led her faculty in creating a remarkable turnaround at an accelerated school, Hollibrook Elementary, outside Houston. She believed that action and accomplishments must be seen in "concrete terms....All staff need to become data collectors" (Still, in Schmoker and Wilson 1993, p. 86).

- Carl Glickman (1993) urges us to ask for "clear indicators: What data or information about effectiveness are currently collected? How complete are the data?... *How does the school community share the data and use them for setting priorities and determining actions?"* (p. 51, emphasis added).

Michael Fullan (1991) not only emphasizes the importance of data to evaluate and monitor progress and monitor results, he also stresses the role of data gathering:

> Gathering data...is also crucial. The success of implementation is highly dependent on the establishment of effective ways of getting information on how well or poorly change is going in the school or classroom (p. 87).

Stressing the connection between teamwork and analysis of data, Fullan adds that "the crux of the matter is getting the right people together with the right information at their disposal" (1991, p. 87). Goals are implicit in this scheme. But local information and data that inform our collaborative effort to reach our goals are essential.

Part of the reason we dismiss this call for data is the outworn mind-set that because schools are so different from other organizations, quality and learning will thrive spontaneously, without any formal effort to use data equivalent to what other organizations use routinely. Schools generally avoid goals and precise means of measuring progress toward them.

We typically hesitate to use data as signposts to assess where we are and where we are headed. Rosenholtz (1991) found that "despite schools' espoused goals of student learning, principals rarely use data on student achievement to evaluate teachers or to monitor student performance even though such data are frequently available" (p. 16).

Fear of Data and Results

Even though goals positively influence improvement, few schools "measure progress against both the ideal outcome and the actual baseline." Such data promote conflict, revealing inconsistencies among teachers and between intent and actual results (Evans 1993, p. 23).

Why do we avoid data? The reason is fear—of data's capacity to reveal strength and weakness, failure and success. Education seems to maintain a tacit bargain among constituents at every level not to gather or use information that will reveal a clear need for improvement: where we need to do better, where we need to make changes. Data almost always point to action—they are the enemy of comfortable routines. By ignoring data, we promote inaction and inefficiency.

Just as Stiggins (1994) saw how fear of retribution may suppress the use of explicit learning goals (see Chapter 2), so, too, can performance data generate fear. This fear helps explain the apparent contradiction between the obvious pleasure that educators would take in improved "achievement results" (Stiggins 1994, p. 64) and their wariness about setting goals that are a necessary precondition for attaining results.

Fatalism feeds fear. Teachers have a limited confidence in their ability to "raise achievement." A few years in the system typically undermines whatever confidence they may have had about their ability to significantly affect groups of children (Lortie 1975, p. 127). This undermining begins even before teachers arrive at school; their professional training does not include closely examining and discussing successful schools or models. Without this training, new teachers arrive tacitly accepting that schools are generally "stuck" institutions, where the only triumphs are personal or infrequent (Lortie 1975, p. 121).

In such a climate, any expectation for improvement seems unrealistic—and generates fear. Teachers regard specific goals as a threat: Will I, can we actually make an impact—a measurable impact? This doubt combines with the fear that failure to reach goals will be used against them. Feedback will be used as evidence that they are failures. "Monitoring results...is frequently misused....In the early attempts at change, people are usually wary of gathering information" (performance data) (Fullan 1991, p. 87). This fear can be seen at every level—from district, to school, to individual classroom teachers. In the classroom, consider the absurdity of the ritual evaluation that teachers undergo; it typically has no connection to what a teacher has or has not accomplished as an individual or a team member. Such a process helps make the "evaluation boondoggle," as Glickman tells us, "perhaps the greatest robbery of educational resources in our time" (1991, p. 7).

This fear of results, of accountability, influenced the impact of outcome-based education (OBE). A majority of schools that set out to respond to the cry to become more outcome based found ways to avoid or postpone becoming results oriented, which was a major part of what "outcome-based" was supposed to mean. Having ever so gingerly put our toes into the cold waters of change, we realized that change would require something like accountability, which we have never warmed toward. We stepped back and took refuge in the much easier and more traditional activity of defining and redefining outcomes—a safer pursuit that waylaid us, like so many things have, on the road to actual improvement.

Reducing Threat from Setting Goals and Using Data

This discussion is not intended to blame anyone; it is aimed at understanding a system that avoids using precise information that can guide and inform better teaching practice. Goal-setting that uses data to monitor progress can be a threatening endeavor. Preparation and ongoing training have often failed to provide teachers with the ability or confidence to believe they can succeed. This insecurity hampers every teacher and administrator, including our most talented and industrious.

We can reduce this threat without eliminating accountability by following some guidelines:

• **Do not use data primarily to identify or eliminate poor teachers.** Such action sends fear throughout the organization and thus encourages avoidance, sabotage, and fudging of data. The usefulness of data is worth more to the best 95 percent of our teachers than to the least effective 5 percent.

- **Do not introduce high stakes prematurely.** Part of the reason that schools in Littleton, Colorado, failed in their attempt to institute OBE was the fear that many students would fail on the new math assessment. Because the assessment had been made a requirement for graduation, parents and students were afraid they would not graduate. Furor replaced reasoned negotiation (Association for Supervision and Curriculum Development 1994).

- **Try to collect and analyze data collaboratively and anonymously by team, department, grade level, or school.** Ensure to the greatest possible extent that those closest to the point of implementation, the practitioners, analyze the data. When possible, let the team exercise its own accountability.

- **Be cautious in implementing pay-for-performance schemes, especially in the beginning**. When data are used for evaluation, institute a "true 'appeal' system,'" which allows schools or teams to "reject, if necessary, targets handed down to them" (Peters 1987, p. 512). Teachers work under difficult conditions, making only a modest amount of collaboration and reflection possible. Peters believes the emphasis should be on measurable progress toward reachable, conservative goals.

- **Allow teachers, by school or team, as much autonomy as possible in selecting the kind of data they think will be most helpful.** The data must accurately reflect teacher *and* student performance and be properly aligned with state, district, and school goals and standards. Establish clear criteria that promote a relevant, substantive focus.

- **Inundate practitioners with success stories that include data.** The stories should stress how measurable success is attainable when we select the right goals—manageable ones—and employ the most effective and proven strategies for reaching them. Here in Colorado, newspaper articles about schools that have made dramatic improvements on the 1998 reading and writing test have inspired other schools to see that "It can be done" and thus to reach for better results.

These measures not only eliminate fear but also promote team spirit and the uninhibited, continuous knowledge-sharing that are the chief benefits of collective effort. Wrongly used, data have a chilling effect. But data can become a force for improvement by energizing those closest to their work. Most of all, data promote the flow of pertinent information and emerging expertise that is the lifeblood of optimism and improvement. Even though teachers are initially wary of gathering data, something quite different takes over when the right kind of improvement process is under way:

> Teachers and others close to implementation are those most insistent on gathering and examining the results of their efforts. Good change processes develop trust and the desire to get better results (Fullan 1991, p. 87).

Data and results can be a powerful force for generating an intrinsic desire to improve. Properly done, "accountability and improvement can be effectively interwoven, but it requires great sophistication" (Fullan 1991, p. 87). Such effort means making accountability more friendly and nonthreatening. A concern with results and improvement can satisfy and energize every constituent, from the practitioner, to the parent, to the school board.

People want—and need—to realize progress toward meaningful goals. Csikszentmihalyi tells about a factory worker whose goal is to complete his assembly-line duties with ever-greater speed and efficiency—one second at a time. For him work is "more fun than watching television" (1990, p. 159). Centennial Elementary School teachers also demonstrate the energizing effect of reaching goals using data:

> Cheers go up as groups plot improvement on the graphs and charts posted around the room. Colleagues share high fives because they have not only reached goals, but have exceeded them. Staff members share an enthusiasm and focus that simply did not exist in the school before (Andrade and Ryley 1992, p. 22).

Goal-orientation. Focus. Enthusiasm. Is this work or play? At Mesa Verde Elementary, measurable gains during the school year resulted in high levels of enthusiasm and desire for more improvement. After seeing the data at an evening meeting, one teacher called another at home; the news could not wait until the next morning. Performance data and feedback—forms of results—nourish that sense of forward movement that is the enemy of boredom. We must establish the right conditions for data to be regarded as useful tools, overcoming that initial wariness and building trust.

Group Data Versus Conventional Data

Collective pride and enthusiasm are the result of an organized effort to monitor and adjust progress based on data. Interestingly, one of the first things we hear when the subject of data is brought up is,

"We already collect data. We always have." To be sure, teachers do have data, such as Individual Education Plans (IEPs), grades, grade-point averages, and test scores. Though such individual data are useful, they are seldom converted into the kind of *group* data that is necessary for more formal and collective reflection and analysis. Even such easily gathered, conventional data are seldom collectively analyzed to help teams or schools find better ways to address collective problems. They could be.

Teachers tend to evaluate students individually and reflect on how to improve class performance less frequently. "We would expect," writes Lortie (1975), "to find heavy emphasis on results attained with classes," as opposed to results with individual students. But only 29 percent of those teachers whom he studied "mentioned generalized outcomes with entire classes" as a source of pride (p. 127). Lortie found that educators do not seek to identify and address patterns of success and failure, which can have broad and continuous benefits for greater numbers of children. Not focusing on patterns is unfortunate, because the real power of data emerges when they enable us to see—and address—patterns of instructional program strengths or weaknesses, thus multiplying the number of individual students we can help.

Lortie (1975) discovered that despite the absence of concern with group outcomes, most teachers did embrace the ideal of "reaching *all* students" (p. 131). But a stark disparity between this ideal and an acceptance of something less than the ideal was apparent. Teachers usually spoke about success in terms of having reached a single student or small group and did not presume that they could have a more general influence. He wonders if teacher training, which emphasizes the individual child, has left teachers "unprepared to think about measurements for *groups* of children?" (p. 128).

We are passing up one of education's greatest unexploited opportunities. If leadership provided the encouragement and opportunity for practitioners to begin gathering and examining collective student results, we would make real strides toward understanding our strengths and weaknesses. A regular examination of collective or aggregate analysis (e.g., the number of students at or above standard) not only promotes a common goal-orientation but also brings forth the insights of many minds. Such analysis breaks down the cellular structure of schools and furnishes a precious perspective that can only be heard in communion with others whose struggles are similar. Group data maximize our ability to develop the most effective improvement and corrective action and to focus that action on the highest-priority areas, those with the greatest opportunity for helping the greatest number of students. If we want many students to benefit from our efforts, we must work to solve the problems that they face. Such patterns and priorities do not emerge spontaneously; rather, they require formal, though not time-consuming, collection and analysis. Some teams in the Amphitheater district made steady progress toward goals by meeting monthly or quarterly for only about 30 minutes (see Appendix). A team leader at one elementary school pointed out that she can gather and chart the data in about 15 minutes. Then the team can discuss what is and is not working and how to get better results the next time.

Data: Making the Invisible Visible

You cannot fight what you cannot see. A group of teachers at one of our schools could not see that student difficulty in demonstrating mathematical processes in writing was a problem of the greatest magnitude until the teachers gathered data using a math rubric they had developed. Very little discussion was necessary at that point. Five minutes of brainstorming generated 10 concrete improvement strategies, three of which became their focus for the next month. The next month's results? Twenty percent more students could reach proficiency in this skill. Data enable us to make efficient use of even brief opportunities for collaboration.

Data make the invisible visible, revealing strengths and weaknesses that are easily concealed. Data promote certainty and precision, which increases teachers' confidence in their abilities. In their studies, both Lortie and Rosenholtz observed a high degree of "teacher uncertainty" (Lortie 1975, p. 132; Rosenholtz 1991, p. 69). Clear goals and ways to assess progress toward them were highly effective in reducing this uncertainty (Rosenholtz 1991). Most schools are not organized to see the connection between effort and accomplishment.

In many organizations, the employees' vague sense that they are not having a meaningful impact can impede progress (Senge 1990). "Tangibility" is the word Lortie (1975) uses to describe a concrete sense that one is making a difference (p. 126). He illustrates its meaning by contrasting an athletic coach's sense of accomplishment with a win-loss record (tangibility) to teachers' vague sense that their efforts benefit students. Performance data gathered and analyzed by a team, group, or faculty not only break down isolation and promote meaningful sharing, they also reveal the impact teachers are having—or not having. Such activity feeds goal-oriented effort as well as personal pride and satisfaction. Data and feedback, forms of results, are the primary ingredients for promoting sustained effort toward goals:

FIGURE 3.2

Mesa Verde Elementary Writing Data: 1994–95

Percentage of students writing at the exiting grade-level standard:

August '94:	12%
November '94:	32%
January '95:	41%
March '95:	51%
May '95:	73%

Note: Increase since August: 61%; student population: 652.

> We assert...that goal-setting activities accentuate those instructional objectives toward which teachers should aim their improvement efforts; that principals, through their frequent monitoring of teachers' progress, specify improvement needs and mobilize school resources (Rosenholtz 1991, pp. 6–7).

Rosenholtz found these elements to be rare in the 78 schools she studied.

Once goals are established, teachers can monitor progress, and goals and data can begin to exert a positive influence. Combined with collaboration, goals and data create conditions that "enable if not compel individual teachers to request and offer advice in helping their colleagues" (Rosenholtz 1991, p. 6). This conformity constrains absolute autonomy, which Rosenholtz found prevalent in the least-effective schools. As Peters and Waterman (1982) have pointed out, conforming to communal norms not only promotes productivity but can be positive and pleasurable.

Common goals that are regularly evaluated against common measures—data—sustain collective focus and reveal the best opportunities for practitioners to learn from each other and hence to get better results. At Mesa Verde Elementary School, data on writing improvement revealed students' pace and progress, which enabled teachers to begin focused, productive dialogue. During the first year that improvements were instituted, the number of students writing at or above grade level rose from 12 percent in August to 32 percent in November, schoolwide. Between November and January, scores rose again, to 41 percent; between January and March, to 51 percent (see Figure 3.2). By May, 73 percent of the students were writing at or above grade level. At one meeting I attended, teachers generated numerous concrete ideas to promote success and address difficulties. Several are included here:

- Model the writing process by having the entire class compose an essay and write it on the board.
- Ask students who are strong in one area to help others who are having trouble in that area.
- Help students brainstorm lists of topics that interest them so that they can draw from the lists when asked to write.

Revealing Where Improvement Is Needed

We must take advantage of data's capacity to prompt collaborative dialogue. Deming saw, like few others, that measurement had power for revealing opportunities for improvement and hence for generating ideas and releasing energy in the service of quality. Data allow the essential points of "leverage" (Senge 1990, p. 114) to emerge, where concealed challenges and opportunities are put in vivid relief:

- John Goodlad's famous study (1984) showed that more than 90 percent of what students do in a normal day consists of boring, passive activities (Fiske 1992).
- Only 11 percent of school districts nationwide disaggregate data to ensure that they can see and thus address the needs of their lowest-achieving populations (Bullard and Taylor 1993).
- According to one study, 90 percent of teachers had never visited another teacher's classroom to observe them and then to "discuss what they could learn from each other" (Glickman 1991, p. 7).
- Second grade teachers at Donaldson Elementary School in our district reviewed stories that 2nd graders had written and discovered that only about 5 of 90 students could write a satisfactory descriptive setting. Effective settings became a priority.
- National Assessment of Educational Progress data reveal that only 3 percent of students nationwide are proficient writers (Olson 1994a).

Objections

Data can convey the magnitude of a problem; they can arrest our attention, establish our priorities, and reveal progress that motivates and sustains us in our efforts. Nonetheless, there are objections to their use.

Schools are not automobile plants; schools cannot control the variables that affect data and outcomes. Many feel that data speak of hard facts in a seemingly "soft" world—that of schools. An automobile plant and a school have significant distinctions: Students are not raw material that we can select or discard; learning is a far less rigid—and therefore less measurable—commodity than automobiles.

This type of thinking may reflect the old fatalism, which prevails in a system that so infrequently cites and seeks to understand the most successful schools, programs, and practices. We sell ourselves short. We *can* influence variables that affect outcomes. The educational system, which includes preservice training, staff development, and teacher induction, needs to disseminate and study success both within and beyond our own schools and districts. We need to learn from successful schools and teachers who have acted on practices that have the highest probability for improved results. For example, a teacher at Canyon Del Oro High School in Tucson, Arizona, implemented a sound, research-based approach to reading instruction to improve the performance of her 33 Chapter I students (Carbo 1986). In four months (*one semester*), the results were impressive:

- One student's reading level improved 4.1 years.
- Six students gained between 3 and 4 years.
- Eight students gained between 2 and 3 years.
- Ten students gained between 1 and 2 years.

Similarly, the Success for All program has raised reading scores dramatically in many of the schools where it was implemented. Improvements typically start in the first year (Slavin, Madden, Dolan, Wasik, Ross, and Smith 1994). Such successes make talk about deficient "raw material" seem irrelevant. They certainly force us to reconsider the inevitability that is implicit in the notion that "the character of a school's output depends largely on the school's input, namely the characteristics of the entering children" (Sarason 1982, p. 268). This statement was probably true in a majority of cases when it was written, but evidence now abounds that ordinary teachers can do extraordinary things—or at least realize incremental improvement with all kinds of "raw material."

We don't have time to be statisticians. Many presume that data come from the statistical arena, that teachers will be forced to master difficult or arcane formulas and thus add yet another time-consuming element to an already crowded schedule. Some consultants and educators inadvertently foster this notion. The reigning perception is that collecting and analyzing data are tantamount to calculating statistics, which is a highly specialized endeavor best left to experts. In reality, only an occasional need for using sophisticated statistical formulas arises. And for those times, experts should be used. But using data does not always require an expert to tell teachers if they have done well. Most data require only the ability to count and calculate percentages. Any conscientious teacher or team of teachers can do this.

I had lunch with an engineer who had participated in many different TQM improvement efforts in industry. I asked him how frequently employees needed to use sophisticated formulas to track progress. He said seldom—if ever. A walk through Allied Signal Corporation in Tucson, Arizona (whose stock has tripled since they instituted continuous improvement procedures), shows a pervasive interest in data. On the wall in every department is a colorful column chart or scatter diagram made with a ruler and felt markers. Most showed monthly progress relative to such simple goals as increasing the number of quality products produced or decreasing the number of defects per thousand. Gathering these data and updating the charts take minimal time.

Tom Peters calls such "back-of-the-envelope" calculations the real tools for improvement. Companies such as the successful GM-Toyota NUMMI plant in California do not use "complex measurement techniques" (Peters 1987, p. 483). Cheap and simple tools, such as pencils and chalk, work fine. Interestingly, the examples of progress in Mary Walton's books (1986, 1990), detailing the success of so many TQM efforts, are similarly simple: a reduction in the number of days or hours needed to complete a process or deliver a product; a reduction in the amount of employee turnover; and the amount of time or money saved. Examples of such simple data and calculations can also be found in education:

• Teachers at George Westinghouse Vocational and Technical School in inner-city Brooklyn enjoyed simply calculated triumphs when they reduced the amount of class cutting by 39 percent and decreased the amount of students failing every class by 92 percent.

• Centennial Elementary School does nothing more than plot monthly the percentage of students who are writing proficiently and put the data on handmade bar graphs. Teachers at one of our middle schools, La Cima, plotted the percentage decrease in such behavioral areas as violent fights, incidents of classroom disruption, bus conduct, and unexcused absences—all immediately available on the computer. Their efforts resulted in significant decreases in six of seven areas.

These kinds of data are neither complex nor time consuming to collect and graph. As the examples demonstrate, there are many simple, time-efficient ways for any teacher or team of teachers to gather and display data.

Data can help us confront what we may wish to avoid and what is difficult to perceive, trace, or gauge; data can substantiate theories, inform decisions, impel action, marshal support, thwart misperceptions and unwarranted optimism, maintain focus and goal-orientation, and capture and sustain collective energy and momentum. Data help us answer the primary question "What do we do next?" amid the panoply of competing opportunities for action. Systems theorist Peter Senge refers to what he calls the greatest point of "leverage," where effort will have the greatest benefit (1990, p. 114). To find these points of leverage, we must continue to ask challenging questions:

- What are data telling us? What problems or challenges do they reveal?
- What can we do about what data reveal? What strategies should we brainstorm? What research should we consult?
- What are data telling us about how effective our current efforts are in helping us to achieve our goals?

Data can be effective tools for promoting improvement. They will never be totally accurate or reliable, but in the hands of conscientious professionals, they promote successful, goal-oriented effort. We cannot afford to indulge in a sophomoric skepticism that absolves us of the responsibility to look at and act on information that tells us how well or not well we are doing.

Successes: Cause for Celebration

Collecting and analyzing data show schools how they are progressing toward improving their practice. The following successes illustrate how data create occasions to celebrate palpable progress.

At the end of the movie *Stand and Deliver,* Jaime Escalante's character is walking down a corridor of Garfield High School in east Los Angeles. He has just discovered that 18 of his students—a record number—have passed the AP Calculus exam. The year is 1982. The movie screen shows his subsequent successes:

- 1983, 30 of his students passed the exam.
- 1984, 63 passed the exam.
- 1985, 77 passed the exam.
- 1986, 78 passed the exam.
- 1987, 87 passed the exam.

These numbers vividly represent Escalante's accomplishments. They add a dimension to a bland statement like "Jaime Escalante is a good teacher." Escalante said that this information enables him to adjust and improve the following year.

At Central Park East, college attendance is an explicit priority. Students begin to discuss and make visits to prospective colleges with their teachers during their junior and senior years. Data showed that about 95 percent of the students who attend this school, which is in a predominantly poor neighborhood, attend college.

The Pomperaug Regional School District in Connecticut is proud of the steady gains students have made on performance assessments. Data from 1994–95 show how they compare with students in other Connecticut districts that are in the same socioeconomic category ("educational reference group," or ERG). On performance assessments in math, writing, and reading, at every grade tested (4, 6, and 8), students were either tied with or ahead of their comparison group. Figure 3.3 shows how students in the Pomperaug Regional School District compared to those in other Connecticut school districts in reading (see the 1996 ASCD book, *A Teacher's Guide to Performance-Based Learning and Assessment*, by the Educators in Connecticut's Pomperaug Regional School District 15).

FIGURE 3.3

Percentage of Students Who Attained Performance Assessment Standard in Reading at Connecticut Schools in the Same Socioeconomic Category

| | PERCENT | |
| | Pomperaug Regional School District | Other School Districts |
Grade		
4	64	53
6	73	70
8	79	71

Source: K. Michael Hibbard, assistant superintendent, Pomperaug Regional School District 15, Connecticut.

At Apollo High School, an alternative program in Simi Valley, California, efforts to help alienated students led to significant progress. Before entering the program, 80 percent of the students were using drugs weekly; 80 percent were missing more than 70 percent of their classes; and 30 percent were on probation. After entering the program, 70 percent of the students improved their attendance; the percentage of students using drugs dropped by 60 percent, and only 5 percent were on probation. Eighty-six percent graduated from high school—a remarkable achievement for an alternative program (Greene and Uroff 1989).

The state of Maryland introduced an initiative to promote better writing skills for all students. In a 10-year period, the percentage of students meeting the state standard rose steadily each year—from 47 percent in 1984 to 92 percent in 1994.

Nancie Atwell was a teacher in a small, rural school in Boothbay Harbor, Maine. She worked hard to teach her students to become skilled, versatile writers. In 1985, her 8th graders took Maine's state writing exam. The results are shown below (Atwell 1987):

- 20 percent of her students scored at the 99th percentile.
- Almost half the students scored above the 90th percentile.
- The mean score was at the 87th percentile.

The Johnson City School District in New York State has a national reputation for being focused and data driven. In 1972, 45 to 50 percent of the students were achieving at or above grade level. Six years later, using their outcomes-driven model, the district increased the percent to 70.

Fort Pitt Elementary School is located in urban Pittsburgh. In 1993, only 1 percent of 4th graders and 3 percent of 5th graders scored at or above the national norm in writing on the Metropolitan Achievement Test. One year later, after the school introduced an inquiry-based approach to research projects, 30 percent of 4th graders and 50 percent of 5th graders scored at or above the norm (Hartmann, DeCicco, and Griffin 1994).

A school improvement consortium called the North Carolina Project set out to make science more engaging by introducing a hands-on curriculum. In one year, the percent of students expressing their enthusiasm for science rose from 38 to 87 percent (O'Neil 1992).

Incremental Improvement

Such improvements are encouraging, but data that reveal gradual, less dramatic improvement are just as crucial. According to Jay McTighe, former director of the Maryland Assessment Consortium, schools need to adopt the spirit of "kaizen," a Japanese word that connotes an ongoing spirit of concern with incremental but relentless improvement, however small. The cumulative impact of many small improvements is thus dramatic. Wiggins thinks that collecting and analyzing data frequently help capture this incremental improvement. Without such activities, we may overlook crucial trend data that can affect teacher morale:

> [Teachers will become] insensitive to small gains, which can lead your staff members to conclude that they can't make any difference, no matter what they do (Wiggins 1994a, p. 15).

We can forestall this discouragement in many ways, such as the following:

• quarterly assessment in math or other subject areas (Addison-Wesley now provides cumulative, quarterly math assessments for its textbook series);
   • writing data collected periodically; and
   • running-record or sight-word-mastery data collected monthly or quarterly.

We do not always need to see dramatic progress; steady growth is sufficient for providing psychic satisfaction and a sense of forward movement (Csikszentmihalyi 1990). Numbers, with the power for revealing slow but steady improvement, combat the fatalism prevalent in schools. The antidote for this fatalism is feedback—clear, precise indications that we are moving forward and becoming more capable.

Disseminating and Replicating Data

Data add another important but overlooked dimension to improvement efforts. They enhance our ability to convey and replicate effective methods within or beyond our schools. People are more likely to invest in a program that research has substantiated than in a program that is merely touted as "good" by others. "Good"—we should know by now—can mean almost anything.

In the Carolingian empire of the early middle ages, trade blossomed when a common currency was introduced. Data that communicate clearly to a wide range of audiences can be our "common currency"; they make the degree of success or failure intelligible to others—school teams, an entire faculty, and other districts.

Everyone wants to succeed; the better we communicate and substantiate successes, the more likely others are to adapt or replicate those successes. When we use different languages and data, learning from others becomes increasingly difficult. Common measures of achievement "serve many practical purposes" and "enable us to chart trends in areas that have an impact on everyday existence, to plot progress toward significant goals" (Guthrie 1993, p. 523). Common measures aid not only in reaching long-term goals but also in resolving short-term problems:

> [Common measures] convey complicated information to a wide audience quickly, to reach agreement on controversial issues in a relatively short period of time and...[are] a major asset in plotting and planning (Guthrie 1993, p. 523).

Precision, simplicity, intelligibility—educational conversations need more of these attributes. Of course, we should maintain a healthy skepticism about successes we read and hear about. But doesn't it help to know that those claiming improvement took the trouble to gauge and then communicate the level of success they have had with a strategy or an innovation?

Beyond "Take My Word for It"

A recent article discussed the efficacy of word processors in helping students write better compositions. The article was somewhat helpful, but the most specific evidence it marshaled was that children who typically avoided writing began to write enthusiastically because word processors made them feel as though they were real writers. More precise evidence, such as that measured by a writing rubric or by criteria, would have strengthened the point that word processors are in fact improving student writing. Sometimes, we underestimate the value such data would have for the practitioners we are addressing.

Many innovations have come and gone, based on claims such as one I read recently: "The program works. If you don't believe us, come to _____ and see for yourself." Firsthand observations would be great if we had the time or opportunity. More precise information can save us the trip. A study of the outcome-based movement found that testimonials and narrative descriptions may be inspirational, but they are not a good basis for action (Evans and King 1994).

Educators are hungry for both kinds of details: evidence of exactly how well a method works as well as concrete descriptions of how to make it work (see Schmoker and Wilson 1993). Providing both types helped make *In Search of Excellence* (Peters and Waterman 1982) a landmark book in the history of business literature

Toward a Sane and Reasonable Accountability

Schools should satisfy a community's reasonable expectation that they provide meaningful information on how they are performing. The community deserves evidence that its schools are acting responsibly and in children's best interest. As Michael Fullan tells us, "accountability and improvement can be effectively interwoven" (Fullan 1991, p. 87). Schools in Clovis, California, have enjoyed an excellent local reputation for quality. Clovis educators take accountability seriously—and in stride. This growing, 25,000-student district is marked by exceptional relations between teachers and administration and between schools and the community that the schools work closely with. Long before "site-based management" entered educational parlance, community members were involved in both school and district goal-setting, using measurable data on everything from academic to affective gains—even the development of character (Schmoker and Wilson 1993). The cover of a promotional flyer shows the district's focus on accountability:

> Quality Is a Standard
> Quality Is a Measurable Goal, Not a Vague Sense of Goodness
> Quality Is a Result

The Clovis schools demonstrate how to interweave accountability and improvement. Both depend upon using measurement judiciously. Data make goals meaningful; without data, we will have only the semblance of accountability.

Parents, communities, and local employers want to know not only about a school and its programs but also how well the school is doing. In Amphitheater schools, they display a question on coffee cups, on posters in buildings around the district, and in a prominent place in the board room. It originated with the special education director, John Rose:

> WHAT do we want for our children, and
> HOW do we know if we are getting it?

That question has a reasonable expectation: It presumes that schools, like other organizations, have an obligation to communicate clearly to stakeholders and to teachers how they are doing.

Accountability and Professionalism

Linda Darling-Hammond (Darling-Hammond and Goodwin 1993) is convinced that in key respects, teaching has not yet attained the goals of a profession; therefore, it lacks professional status. Among the prerequisites for a genuine professionalism is "accountability, including the relationship that exists between practitioners and their clients and between practitioners and the society at large" (p. 22). We are not there yet.

If schools, like hospitals, fail to serve their clients by failing to institute the most effective methodologies, then the schools should inform the community. Providing such information is a professional obligation. If, on the other hand, schools systematically and continuously adapt the best that is known and are getting good results, they deserve credit and additional support, which will produce even better results. Accountability should place obligations on the schools as well as on the communities that support them. It may be the necessary price to pay for autonomy: As Edward Fiske points out, "You cannot have *yin* without *yang*. When it comes to the redesigning of America's public schools, you cannot have freedom without accountability" (Fiske 1992, p. 237).

The Common Sense of Teamwork, Goal Setting, and Performance Data

When the three concepts of teamwork, goal setting, and data use interact, they address a misunderstanding prevalent in schools. The misunderstanding is that we can improve without applying certain basic principles: People accomplish more together than in isolation; regular, collective dialogue about an agreed-upon focus sustains commitment and feeds purpose; effort thrives on concrete evidence of progress; and teachers learn best from other teachers. We must ensure that these three concepts operate to produce results.

Do we want schools to continue merely adopting innovations? Or do we want schools to improve? Do we want to merely train personnel in new standards and current methodology? Or do we want to help more students apply mathematical operations; write quality essays; deliver effective oral presentations; and appraise and respond to social, historical, and scientific issues? If we collectively focus on such goals and regularly measure the impact of the methods we are learning from each other, we *will* get better results.

Rapid Results:
The Breakthrough
Strategy

We didn't find any examples in which people focused on something of importance that didn't produce effects in the first year. If the change...is going to affect the kids, it is going to affect them very rapidly.

—Bruce Joyce (cited in Sparks 1998a, p. 34)

The "small, tangible steps" route to strategic breakthroughs is the only implementation strategy I know of that continually delivers dramatic results.

—Peters 1987

Chapters 1–3 discussed the three concepts that are the foundation for improvement: informed, effective teamwork; goal setting; and the use of performance data. This chapter translates these concepts into key strategies for making the foundation work—and work fast. The "breakthrough strategy" focuses on small but immediate improvements and operationalizes and accelerates the effectiveness of teamwork, goals, and data (Schaffer 1988).

If we consistently analyze what we do and adjust to get better, we will improve. School improvements are neither so "exotic, unusual, or expensive that they are beyond the grasp of...ordinary schools" (Clark et al. 1984, p. 59). But this plan hinges on our ability to see the impact of what we are doing. And that impact does not need to be dramatic; continuous, incremental improvements are the real building blocks of sweeping systemic change that is rapid—and attainable.

Most school improvement efforts do not take the "short view" advocated in this chapter. But some do:

- Bessemer Elementary school in Pueblo, Colorado, has an 80 percent free and reduced lunch population. *Between 1997 and 1998,* the percentage of students at or above grade level in reading rose from 12 percent to 64 percent. During the same year, the percentage of students writing at or above standard rose from 2 percent to 48 percent.

- George Westinghouse Vocational and Technical School in downtown Brooklyn reduced the number of students failing every class from 151 to 11—in *one semester.* Teachers reduced class cutting 39 percent—in *six weeks.*

- The transformation of the Johnson City School District began with Superintendent John Champlin's intense efforts at one school. Achievement gains at this school were evident at the end of *one year.*

- At Hawthorne Elementary School, located in a disadvantaged area of Seattle, 32 percent of African American students were achieving in the lowest quartile (the lowest-achieving 25 percent) in 1989. *One year later,* the number was reduced to 19 percent. During that same period, white students in the lowest quartile went from 8 percent to zero (Bullard and Taylor 1993).

- At the University of California at Berkeley, minority students routinely performed at the bottom of their class in college algebra. A teacher, Philip Treisman, set out to improve their grades. He arranged for them to begin meeting to study and assist each other. Their performance *immediately* improved, exceeding their nonminority counterparts in one semester (Steele 1992).

- At Amphitheater Middle School, a new intervention policy was introduced to reduce the number of disciplinary incidents. At the end of *one 9-week quarter,* 95 referrals were written; at the same time the previous year, 250 had been written.

- At La Cima Middle School in our district, teacher teams developed and used high-interest activities and assessments to help prepare students to succeed on the state writing exam. In *four months,* La Cima, with its 42 percent free and reduced-lunch population, tied the most affluent school district in Arizona on the state writing exam.

- At Fort Pitt Elementary School in urban Pittsburgh, only 1 percent of 4th graders and 3 percent of 5th graders scored at or above the national norm on the Metropolitan Writing Exam. After teachers adopted a high-engagement, "guided-inquiry" approach to research projects, writing levels rose to 30 percent in 4th grade and to 50 percent in 5th grade—in *one year.* During the same year, discipline referrals plummeted by 71 percent (Hartmann, DeCicco, and Griffin 1994).

- The North Carolina Project adopted new science materials and teaching methods to make science more engaging and hands-on. Student satisfaction with science classes rose from 38 to 87 percent—in *one year* (O'Neil 1992).

• Highly successful, early-intervention programs, such as Reading Recovery and Success for All, begin to see results almost immediately. Most improvements in reading occur during the *first semester* of implementation and are often most dramatic during the *first and second years* (Slavin et al. 1994).

• In Israel, a study compared history achievement for two groups. The experimental group was taught using a collaborative/group investigation model; the control group continued to be taught using conventional "whole-class" methods. The result: the experimental group achieved gains *two and a half times* that of their whole-class counterparts; they even exceeded the performance of the more advantaged group—in *one year* (Joyce, Wolf, and Calhoun 1993, p. 66).

In each of these cases, schools established collective goals, tracked them using data, then used the data to assess or adjust efforts toward better results. These are the essential ingredients we examined in the first three chapters.

But these rapid successes also reflect the judicious selection of goals that can be reached in a reasonable time. An intensive, collaborative focus on selected goals increases the chance for immediate impact. Joyce, Wolf, and Calhoun (1993) found that "where significant improvement has happened, it has happened rapidly.... Innovations can be implemented and gains seen in student achievement within a year." They insist, in what sounds presumptuous if not heretical in today's climate, that the key is to "pay attention to already existing approaches that work and work fast" (p. 52).

Good News: Room for Improvement

Historically, the quality of education in the United States has been among the best in the world. We have provided an education to record numbers of students over time. But this accomplishment may obscure the current need and opportunity to improve. Although we work hard, we must remember Deming's admonition that "it is possible and in fact fairly easy for an organization to go downhill even though everyone in the organization performs with devotion" (Deming 1986, p. 26). Our educational system fails to work "smarter, not harder," thus limiting improvement opportunities.

Like most organizations, U.S. schools can improve without adding significant time to the school day. Schaffer (1988) explains the reasoning behind this statement by making a radical assumption: Most organizations are only performing between 40 and 60 percent of their capacity.

My experience as an English teacher supports this assumption. During seven years of teaching, I regularly assigned writing activities and required that students read and discuss a variety of texts. But I did little to encourage what could have improved their writing ability: establishing writing criteria and offering opportunities for prewriting, peer editing, and immediate feedback. And I also wasted time by meticulously grading papers that weren't even going to be revised and by scribbling extensive notes over the papers. These practices were ineffective—even harmful (Marzano and Arthur 1977). As a teacher, I was probably operating at 40 to 60 percent capacity—if that.

Evidently, my experience was not isolated; most classrooms lack even the most basic teaching processes crucial to good writing (Rothman 1992b). This lack may help explain a recent National Assessment of Educational Progress report on student writing: "No more than 3 percent of students at any grade level were able to write an 'elaborated' or better response" (Olson 1994a). About 73 percent of 4th grade writing samples received low ratings (Jones 1995).

If we had spent even 20 minutes of our monthly department meetings discussing research on what good writing should be, or which methods promoted good writing, many feckless practices might have been replaced with more effective (not to mention time-saving) methods.

The English department at Amphitheater High School exemplifies how teachers can combine teamwork, goals, and data to operate at their capacity. Their efforts resulted in steady improvement in the quality of student introductions in written work. Department members met regularly to identify and track key difficulties students were having. They then shared and generated new interventions and materials to help students move toward their goal of becoming better writers.

There is room for improvement in many areas, as the following examples illustrate:

- **Science**. Science curriculum and textbooks cover almost three times more topics than those of our international counterparts (Schmoker and Marzano 1999). Science texts are dull, emphasizing too much vocabulary and memorization. This approach guarantees shallow coverage. "Despite calls for curricular reforms that emphasize 'doing' science, lectures and textbook use continue to dominate science instruction" (Rothman 1992a, p. 15). We should not be surprised then that most students find high school biology "boring or irrelevant" (*ERS Bulletin* 1990, p. 4).

- **Math.** Research on a national math test reveals that only 18 percent of 4th graders, 25 percent of 8th graders, and 16 percent of 12th graders can perform at the "proficient" level (O'Neil 1993). In the 8th and 12th grades, there are disturbing gaps between U.S. achievement and that of our international counterparts (U.S. Department of Education 1998).

- **Inadequate Teacher Induction.** In Japan and Korea, the law requires that new teachers spend about 20 days during their first year learning the art of teaching from a mentor teacher. In the United States, "supervised induction to teaching is ad hoc or nonexistent" (Darling-Hammond and Goodwin 1993, p. 33).

- **Underfunded Staff Development.** School districts typically spend less than 1 percent of their annual budget on training (Bullard and Taylor 1993). Underfunding at the school level reflects what Deming found on a broader scale: "In its underuse and abuse of talent, America is the most underdeveloped country in the world" (1986, p. 6).

- **Lack of Student Engagement.** Lounsbury and Clark (1990) conducted a nationwide study of 162 middle schools. Years into the middle school movement, which emphasized active learning, they observed a "dominance of passive learning." Most 8th graders "have resigned themselves to the fact that classes are boring" (pp. 136–137). Although we know that students must be engaged in learning to retain and apply it (Wolfe and Sorgen 1990, Newmann 1992), we continue to provide the least engaging kind of curriculum for rural and inner-city students who need the most help (Haberman 1990).

- **Poor Instructional Leadership.** Less than 10 percent of school principals are "systematic problem solvers" (Leithwood and Montgomery 1986). Studies of school leadership show that "the average school administrator…simply reflects on lesser things than the purpose of schooling and curriculum and instruction issues" (Smith and Andrews 1989, p. 4).

- **No Criteria or Expectations Given to Students.** We have discovered that students perform better when we provide them with the criteria we expect them to meet and give them models, examples, and "anchor papers" that specify our expectations (Hillocks 1987, Wiggins 1994a, Stiggins 1994). As Sizer (1992), Wiggins (1994a), and Stiggins (1994) have been telling us, this area is a huge and overlooked opportunity for us to improve.

- **Failure to Reach Children in Poverty.** Only 11 percent of all districts nationwide disaggregate student data to determine how to raise the achievement of the lowest-achieving populations (Bullard and Taylor 1993). We do not address the dismaying fact that, generally, students from low socioeconomic categories are still performing well below their peers (Singham 1998). The reason is not solely socioeconomic conditions. Unfortunately, those who teach in rural and urban areas characteristically use retrograde and ineffective instructional methods that are not based on research (Haberman 1990).

The problems in these areas point to a large gap between what we know and what we do. How wide is this gap? Joyce, Wolf, and Calhoun (1993) provide some idea:

> Of the 20 or more most powerful teaching strategies that cross subject areas and have a historical track record of high payoff in terms of student effects, we speculate that fewer than 10 percent of us—kindergarten through university level—regularly employ more than one of these strategies (p. 38).

Based on his studies, Edmonds (1979) concludes that "there isn't a single educational problem that doesn't have a solution"; "we can, wherever and whenever we choose, successfully teach all children whose schooling is of interest to us" (p. 23). We can close the gap between what we know and what we do by improving incrementally:

- Increase the number of students who can write—and enjoy writing—quality persuasive essays.
- Increase our staff development budget from the current $\frac{1}{2}$ to 1 percent. Even that additional $\frac{1}{2}$ percent, properly targeted, can make a difference.
- Ensure that relevant and engaging learning occurs with increasing frequency.
- Create expectations and promote training and conditions that help principals focus more time and energy on helping solve the most pressing school problems—one at a time.
- Increase the number of low-achieving students who can achieve at higher levels.

Schools may have more potential for immediate improvement than many other organizations. Why? Because, as outlined in Chapter 3, they suffer from the most crippling weaknesses: They are uniquely cellular, goal-averse, and dataphobic—more so than perhaps any other kind of organization (Lortie 1975, Rosenholtz 1989).

The Need for a Breakthrough:
Doing More with What We Have

Such opportunities for improvement make Schaffer's break-through strategy especially applicable to schools. It helps clarify what some have known for years: There is a marked difference between vague, well-intentioned improvement efforts and carefully targeted, goal-oriented, short-term efforts aimed explicitly at getting measurable, *substantive* results quickly. The former characterizes the disappointing failures of the past; the latter can achieve better short-term and long-term results. This strategy requires leadership that any dedicated administrator can provide; it does not require immediate and vast increases in resources.

Although change is always "resource-hungry" (Fullan 1991, p. 64), resources can be found as well as made. If we can achieve better results by making better use of what we have, we can make a more compelling case for additional funding. Unfortunately, new money seldom raises achievement, a pattern that is obvious to the public (Odden, Monk, Nakib, and Picus 1995). People in the United States are ready to spend more money on education. But they want "some assurance that they are not pouring money down a bottomless hole" (President Clinton, in Fiske 1992, p. 276). Because most schools are so poorly organized for improvement, we can leverage existing resources and personnel to achieve more. Employees at every level are usually convinced that they are producing as much as anyone can with existing resources (Schaffer 1988). But as business and education studies have shown, we can do better.

Success is a function of organizing, marshaling, and implementing great ideas and making a commitment to improvement. Armed with organized intelligence and optimism, the sky's the limit. General Electric CEO Jack Welch has been called the "world's greatest business leader." He ascribes GE's success to its belief in its "infinite capacity to improve anything," that

> There is, in fact, unlimited juice in that lemon.... [Improvement] is about tapping an ocean of creativity, passion, and energy that as far as we can see, has no bottom and no shores (Lowe 1998, p. 108).

Schaffer's (1988) bedrock principle, that most of us are performing at between 40 and 60 percent of our capacity, defines the opportunity implicit in the breakthrough strategy:

> Locating and starting at once with the gains that can be achieved quickly, and then using those first successes as stepping-stones to increasingly ambitious gains (p. 13).

Among the most promising and enlightened school reform movements of the last decades is the Coalition of Essential Schools. Now, many years into its reform effort, the movement appears to be moving slower than originally anticipated. An article in *Phi Delta Kappan* gave a somber assessment of the movement's progress by concluding that "there are no quick fixes or miracle cures. For all their high hopes that it would be 'the reform that's going to make the difference,'" the coalition now "would like to temper this enthusiasm" (Muncey and McQuillan 1993, p. 487). Plenty of process, plenty of time. But not much in the way of results.

Or consider the late Al Shanker's (1994) frustrated take on school reform in Chicago. Shanker, who was president of the American Federation of Teachers, was eager to see how their schools were progressing. After seven years of school reform, school officials there told him that new initiatives "were making a tremendous difference." He arrived to find "no data or discussion about student performance," only "enthusiastic quotes from students and teachers." He concluded that Chicago's primary problem is that after all these years, the district never made any real "attempt to measure progress toward the goal of improved student achievement and an analysis of what seems to be working and what seems to be failing" (p. 43). Fortunately, under the leadership of Superintendent Paul Vallas in the late 1990s, Chicago schools are getting measurably better results.

Compare these reforms with the history of the Success for All reading program. The chief difference is that Success for All focused immediately on results—in both the short and long term—in specific areas of achievement. It has realized them in the course of becoming one of the fastest-growing, most successful programs in the history of education. Using data and feedback from ongoing field studies, the program's founders have adjusted and improved the program into one that usually gets results *during the first year of implementation*. The results speak for themselves.

Most reforms are not failing for lack of intelligence, effort, or industry. The problem may be that we are too patient. We could be seeing steady, palpable progress, as measured by any number of viable assessments and indicators and by setting a limited number of substantive but realistic and measurable short-term goals.

Impatience Is a Virtue: The Importance of Short-Term Goals

In "results-driven programs,...the mood is one of impatience. Management wants to see results now, even though the change process is a long-term commitment" (Schaffer and Thomson 1992, p. 83).

Immediately focusing on processes as they affected results was at the core of the success that effective TQM companies experienced. The stories contained in journalist Mary Walton's books (1986, 1990) on measurably successful TQM efforts attest to this focus. Brian Joiner, Deming's close associate, also urges us to "make sustained, rapid improvement a way of life."

Nonetheless, for most business consultants, it was "near-anathema to suggest any focus on results" (Brigham 1994, p. 22). Business people still hear that slowness is a virtue and that results will automatically accrue if companies adopt the Total Quality philosophy and practices—and have patience (Brigham 1994).

Results-oriented planning and measurement promote the successes that add hope to the apparent futility of large-scale reform attempts. Short-term success, even "purposeful impatience," sustains the essential interest and energy to persevere (Fullan 1991, p. 83). Not to mention that short-term, incremental gains in learning are eminently achievable.

Psychological Benefits of Short-Term Results

The most effective TQM companies are obsessed with short-term results—and they get them. Evidence and case studies show that schools can also improve rapidly. Impatience is central to this improvement; a wrong-headed patience overlooks a psychological need for feedback, a need that is seldom met in today's workplace. Employees "perceive their psychic rewards to be scarce, erratic, and unpredictable" (Lortie 1975, p. 212). This situation may help explain why "disenchantment is rampant" among veteran teachers, who constitute about 70 percent of the teaching force (Evans 1989, p. 10).

We underestimate the importance of urgency and how fast it dissipates after the initial fanfare. Chang, Labovitz, and Rosansky (1992) think that we should "demand short-term results," and that impatience can be used to our advantage:

> In the real world people aren't very patient. They find it difficult to work hard at something when they're told the results won't be visible for months or even years. That's why we advise our clients to demand short-term results from their long-term TQM process. We advocate what we call the "Quick-Start" Approach (p. 102).

As previously mentioned, teachers at Thunderbolt Middle School in Lake Havasu implemented the Accelerated Reader Program. By meeting regularly and reviewing performance data, they were able to see results *by the end of the first quarter.* By the end of December, it was evident that their students were on course to significantly exceed the previous year's reading performance.

Periodic Data

Writing is one of several excellent areas to promote "quick wins in target areas." Measurable progress in students' writing can convince practitioners of the value of collaboration and ongoing, periodic assessment and data analysis. Scoring guides provide common language for productive discussion. If teachers conduct writing assessments on a predetermined schedule, they can quickly determine the percentage of students writing at or above an established standard. Their task is to simply identify which criteria in the rubric is giving the greatest number of students difficulty; to discuss or brainstorm for ways to more effectively teach to that area of weakness, and then to implement the new strategy. At the next meeting, the percentage of students writing more effectively is almost bound to go up, reflecting the power of the strategies being shared and refined at the regular meetings.

As we have seen, this same approach can be taken with periodic running records, with math assessments, or with student behavior data as teachers meet to evaluate their progress, to target areas for improvement, and to test new strategies against subsequent results. Johnson City High School set out to help more students pass the New York Regents Competency exam in Mathematics. They realized a dramatic increase when they began to administer quarterly assessments and then to analyze the results.

This analysis can be an enormously satisfying, energizing process for teachers who have traditionally been deprived of seeing the effect of their collective efforts on student learning. It was an encouraging revelation for the principal and faculty at Havasupai Elementary School in Lake Havasu City, Arizona, when teacher Nyana Sims provided them with data that showed significant quarterly increases in the percentage of students making adequate progress in reading. It nicely foreshadowed the exceptional year-end results they achieved and gave them something to celebrate.

If we want to improve, then we need positive, short-term feedback. Even though "certain activities require a very long time to accomplish,...the components of goals and feedback are still very important" (Csikszentmihalyi 1990, p. 55). Reaching short-term goals provides "joy," which once experienced, makes us want more (Csikszentmihalyi 1990, p. 42). Anticipating short-term benefits energizes the improvement process and keeps it from bogging down in easier, more conventional activities that do not directly affect student results.

Activity-Centered Programs Versus Results-Driven Programs

Educators tend to postpone a concern with ends—with results—perhaps because "means-end relationships in teaching are not well understood" (Lortie 1975, p. 212). Such action is painfully apparent at many educational conferences, where we hear cursory or clichéd descriptions of activities conducted, partnerships formed, and committees established, without any reference to a single result. This endless train of preparation and activities has been called the "rain dance":

> [The rain dance is] the ardent pursuit of activities that sound good, look good, and allow managers to feel good—but in fact contribute little or nothing to bottom-line performance. These activities, many of which parade under the banner of "total quality" or "continuous improvement"…[reflect] a fundamentally flawed logic that confuses ends with means, processes with outcomes (Schaffer and Thomson 1992, p. 80).

Compare this definition to a description of the dismal state of high school reform, where after more than a decade, "there is a lot of activity but there is not a clear vision as to what is necessary....We're not making much progress" (Viadero 1994, p. 1).

As we have seen, Glickman (1993) discovered that activities can become the goal. In other words, many organizations are "equating measures of activities with actual improvement of performance" (Schaffer and Thomson 1992, p. 84). Such measures have a legitimate use, but not when they ignore student learning results.

"Perpetual Preparations": A Waste of Time and Money

"Perpetual preparations" are not only ineffective, they also "waste billions" (Schaffer 1988, p. 39). In the name of patience, many initiatives get so bogged down in endless planning that they "have disappeared in the implementation" (Joyce, Wolf, and Calhoun 1993, p. 6).

I had a conversation with a consultant who had worked intensively with a number of schools for several years. "Any results?" I asked her.

"Oh no," she replied. These efforts are "still evolving." It was "much too early to expect results." Even, I asked her, for the schools where she had worked for three or more years?

"It's premature," she said. They are still "laying the foundation."

Another telling example is one state's 6-year-old reform effort. Even though much expense and activity went toward establishing site-based school councils, the new performance-based assessment program "resulted in only modest changes in teachers' instructional practices." One review found that the "vast majority of teachers" were "frozen in virtually the same instructional patterns" (Guskey 1994, p. 53). Another review found that "the idea that the ultimate purpose of councils is to advance student learning has not been stressed enough" (David 1994, p. 711).

If we set out to establish site councils, we will establish site councils; we will not improve schools.

If we set specific goals and honestly and systematically commit ourselves to achieving them, we will almost invariably improve.

From Early Momentum to Systemic Change

The preceding examples are not the exception; they are the rule. Current organizational habits that avoid focusing on short-term, measurable gains are the major obstacles impeding not only isolated improvements but also systemwide transformation. Palpable gains are the key to leveraging change in the system because they can unravel the "tangle of debilitating patterns that are reinforced by formal and informal institutional mechanisms" (Schaffer 1988, p. 19). Impatience itself can begin to transform the system. Lee Iaccoca once directed his staff to develop a prototype for a convertible. When they enthusiastically responded that they could have one in about nine months, he bellowed, "You just don't understand. Go find a car and saw the top off the damned thing" (Iaccoca, in Peters 1987, p. 253).

Schaffer (1988) cites the example of Domino Sugar, where in just six weeks, problem-solving teams reduced bag breakage by 80 percent and overfill by 56 percent. They achieved the reductions by multiplying brainpower through team problem solving, not by adding resources. This one improvement led to systemwide changes in every department in the refinery.

It also changed the system. Based on these reductions, the improvement was implemented at other plants, where it produced results and also broke down age-old barriers between union and management. Initial skepticism gave way to enthusiasm and cooperation: At first "no one really wanted to own the project—that is until we started to get results. Then everyone got excited and wanted to get into the act" (Schaffer 1988, p. 107).

"Early momentum can mean the difference between a rapid sequence of successes that sustains momentum and a mere plodding along...and no palpable excitement." The need for early, rapid successes indicates that "pilot projects that are selected during the planning stages must have high probability for quick success and meaningful impact" (Brigham 1994, pp. 45–46). It is crucial that we carefully establish concrete, achievable "short-term subgoals." Otherwise, people are unrealistically expected to "maintain a high effort as they slog toward goals they can only attain months or even years later." Such work "may afford team members only a single reinforcing moment of success" (Schaffer 1988, p. 31).

Lortie (1975) saw this 20 years ago: A teacher who felt pride because all her students could read by the end of the year, remarked that "the rest of the year I'm wondering" (p. 127).

"Quick Wins in Target Areas"

The key in the early going is to select the right projects. According to an A.T. Kearney report, newcomers applying TQM should select pilot projects that "promote early successes on substantial issues" (Brigham 1994, p. 46). Schaffer and Thomson (1992) maintain that success starts with identifying "quick wins in target areas…initiatives that employees could take right away to generate measurable improvement in a short time" (p. 88).

How can we emulate this success in education? We can select substantive slices—small but meaningful challenges that promote success and hence optimism. As we have seen, in only one year, Centennial Elementary School saw dramatic improvements in students' writing ability. But more important, grade-level teams began to see improvements at the beginning, during monthly meetings.

Expanding Our Vision of What's Possible: The Need for "Zest"

The small starts I describe in this chapter are the seeds of large-scale success. Small, measurable successes, achieved annually, quarterly, or monthly, can release the optimism and enthusiasm—or "zest"—as Schaffer (1988, p. 52) calls it, that may be the most important ingredient in improvement. The breakthrough strategy uses this zest to maintain energy for reaching goals, removing barriers, and increasing confidence:

> The breakthrough strategy attempts to recreate the zest factors—which release so much force and energy in reaching important short-term goals—and uses them as the wedge to break through institutionalized barriers. Immediate successes are essential if people are to increase their confidence and expand their vision of what is possible (p. 60).

Former Amphitheater Superintendent Richard Wilson likens the impact of such success to athletic victories. The difference is that "careful planning can all but ensure small-scale victories. Those victories provide positive reinforcement. With each small win, a team can begin to feel like it is unstoppable—like a steamroller—as each success feeds on itself."

Can we routinely expect such swift and significant change? The answer may be a surprising "yes." The key is to regularly marshal collective intelligence and chart progress toward goals that teachers have agreed upon and that can reveal incremental progress. Established performance rubrics provide such ways. I explore these and other possibilities in Chapter 7.

An atmosphere charged with progress and improved results sustains and energizes people toward effective alternatives to their existing routines. Myriad organizations, schools, and sound psychology show that the process works.

As we have seen, carefully selected, short-term projects can precipitate successful change—and optimism. Much of what accounts for this success is learning about the best that others have studied and discovered. Research, the accumulated, practical knowledge that has been gathered over the last few decades, gives us an added advantage as we seek effective, rapid change. It steers us away from discredited (and therefore time-wasting) practices, while directing us toward best practice. The next chapter explores the role of research and development in the improvement scheme.

5

Research and Development

What we have learned about teaching and learning in the last 15 years is among the most exciting discoveries of our 200-year history.

—Peter Senge

The principles discussed in the preceding chapters were the result of research—formal studies that demonstrate the effectiveness of these principles. But research is not enough; for every item of research we adopt, we must conduct on-site action research. The research we do at the local level—collaboratively—is what makes formal, outside research work. Outside research cannot be installed like a car part—it has to be fitted, adjusted, and refined for the school contexts we work in.

Until we begin to routinely respect and respond to the best that is known about effective teaching and organizational improvement, we forfeit the benefits of the rich knowledge base that can inform our teamwork as we pursue substantive goals. Until we routinely consult this knowledge base, we limit every student and teacher in our system.

When we begin to more systematically close the gap between what we know and what we do, we will be on the cusp of one of the most exciting epochs in the history of education. Most dedicated educators acknowledge this gap, which may be one of the reasons that teaching is still regarded as "the not-quite profession" (Goodlad, in Darling-Hammond and Goodwin 1993, p. 20). As we have seen, Joyce and others (1993) speculate that only the smallest fraction of the best that we know is used routinely by educators from kindergarten through graduate school. Fullan (1994) uses an oxymoron to describe a teacher: a "nonreading professional"; many practitioners do not read what leaders in their field write (p. 246). I am always surprised by the number of teachers in graduate classes I have taught who have never read or heard of publications like *Educational Leadership* or *Phi Delta Kappan*. In such a research-poor context, isolated experience replaces professional knowledge as the dominant influence on how teachers teach (Little 1990).

A kind of pseudo-research has rushed into this breach: reforms that were supposedly informed by research and that promised to dramatically improve the quality of education. But these major reforms, which were implemented on a grand, even nationwide scale, never delivered (Gitlin 1990). We did not hear much evidence that they had achieved results in real-school settings or that students were generally learning more as a result of the reforms. The reforms failed and quietly left the stage. The very word "research" lost vital currency and increasingly now evokes cynicism.

What Research Shows

Yet good research, whether we call it best knowledge or best practice, can unleash vast, dormant forces for making every child's and teacher's life richer and more interesting. Unfortunately, we do not always apply what research shows, as the examples that follow illustrate:

• **Basic Skills and Higher-Order Skills.** We labor under the incorrect notion that students must master basic skills before they can learn higher-order skills or engage in complex activities. Studies in math, reading, and writing clearly demonstrate that the opposite is true: Students learn best when basic skills are taught in a vital, challenging context that makes the skills meaningful. The very thing that keeps students from achieving in these areas is the dry, irrelevant teaching strategies we often employ, especially with students who most need real challenges (Means, Chelemer, and Knapp 1991). Low-performing students stand to gain the most from approaches that incorporate basic skills into complex, higher-order tasks and problems. Schools and effective programs have demonstrated that standardized test scores can improve significantly when challenging tasks and activities are used (Resnick, Bill, Lesgold, and Leer 1991; Schmoker and Wilson 1993; Livingston, Castle, and Nations 1989; Pogrow 1988, 1990).

• **Writing.** The complex skill of writing is still taught in a primitive fashion. Despite research showing the importance of regular practice in writing, it still gets short shrift in the classroom. According to recent National Assessment of Educational Progress data, the average student spends about 30 minutes a week on writing (Jones 1995). An alarming number of students are required to write without the benefit of even the most well-established practices supported by research, such as prewriting and revision (Rothman 1992b). A 1995 story commented on the lamentable state of writing instruction by using words from Shakespeare: "If you have tears, prepare to shed them now" (Jones 1995, p. 18). Too many schools continue to substitute inferior activities for actual reading and writing during the large block of time that is devoted to language arts.

• **Reading.** Research shows that reading itself—lots of it—is perhaps the most vital and worthy activity for students to engage in to improve their reading ability and test scores (Krashen 1993; Showers et al. 1998). Building language instruction around lots of reading and dialogue about that reading (but not excluding phonics and skills instruction) is the best approach, especially after students have learned basic decoding skills (Palincsar and Klenk 1991). In one study, such reading and focused dialogue led to astonishing results: Students' reading scores increased 15 months in 15 days of instruction. Students who had been answering 30 percent of their comprehension questions correctly were now getting 80 percent of them right (Berliner and Casanova 1993, p. 9) .

We overlook a growing body of research showing that early, intensive intervention ensures that students can get a good start in school by leaving 1st grade with the ability to read at grade level. Strategies used in intervention programs, such as Success for All and Reading Recovery, succeed because they incorporate word skill strategies and construct meaning from texts. They also insist on the "regular, ongoing assessment" that is advocated throughout this book (Pikulski 1994, p. 17). Research for these early-intervention strategies is so compelling that companies are beginning to offer money-back guarantees if schools do not see dramatic results. Again, one of the most valuable and productive things we can do is to review our current reading programs in light of the best research and research-based programs. At Havasupai Elementary School, reading scores rose significantly when a team of teachers reviewed the research, made on-site visits to successful program sites, and then thoroughly revamped their early reading program. The rise in scores was immediate and dramatic.

• **Leadership.** Research in business and education demonstrates that leadership is essential to substantive and enduring progress. Yet the literature reveals a lack of strategic leadership that focuses on improving instruction. Studies point instead to the realities of our current system—one in which a principal's day seldom reflects any meaningful influence on what goes on in the classroom (Smith and Andrews 1989). And principals rarely apply systematic approaches to solving school problems: Only about 10 percent of school principals are "systematic problem solvers" (Leithwood and Montgomery, in Fullan 1991, p. 151). This situation is not the principal's fault. Everyone should be responsible for adjusting the current system to increase opportunities, not just to manage but to lead schools toward ever-improving results.

• **Socioeconomic Factors and Achievement.** Socioeconomic factors never have and never will preclude high achievement—for groups or individual children. Numerous studies reveal that a *school's* effectiveness is what promotes high achievement (Goodlad 1975). With the right in-class interventions, traditionally low achievers can significantly out-achieve their high socioeconomic status (SES) counterparts (Joyce, Wolf, and Calhoun 1993; Steele 1992). In their studies, Mortimore and Sammons (1987) found that in reading, school interventions were "about six times more important than background. For written math and writing, the difference is tenfold" (p. 6). How many ambitious plans have we scrapped, how much teacher morale and human potential have we squandered because we unquestionably bought the notion that socioeconomic factors determined students' level of achievement? We should make discussion of this issue one of our first and highest priorities.

• **Cooperative Learning.** One of the more jarring paradoxes in education is the gap between the rich research base on cooperative learning and its unfortunate underuse in the classroom. Though virtually every teacher has acquired some semblance of training in this highly effective method, estimates are that only about 10 percent of teachers use it (Antil et al. 1998). This is especially unfortunate in light of what Bruce Joyce and his associates (Joyce, Weil, and Showers 1992) found: One of the simplest forms of cooperative learning—having students occasionally work in pairs to ensure each other's understanding of difficult concepts—can be expected to bring immediate effects, especially among low-achievers. They also found that such simple pairings are especially effective in helping students to succeed in math and science.

• **Direct Instruction.** Wesley Elementary School in Houston, Texas, is an inner-city school with a population that is 99-percent minority. It has an 82-percent poverty rate. And yet it ranks among the best 12 schools in Houston. First graders place in the 82nd percentile, fully 50 percentile points higher than their socioeconomic counterparts (Nadler 1998). Once again: How long can we continue to assume that socioeconomic status is destiny?

Wesley gets these results by using direct instructional methods: clear, sequenced instruction and feedback provided on an organized schedule. A look at the most effective early reading programs reveals meticulously devised direct instruction to be one of its essential aspects: students facing the teacher, listening to instructions, and responding to questions as they move toward mastery.

This is not to imply that there should be less interaction or discussion in the classroom. But the research on direct instruction shows that, like cooperative learning, it is underused—and not effectively refined through collaborative action research. Teachers could perhaps teach students numerous skills and concepts most effectively—and even engagingly—through direct instructional systems. These systems could be designed by teams of teachers for selected standards and benchmarks.

• **Alignment Among Standards, Instruction, and Assessment.** We have yet to put into operation the simple principle that for improvement to occur, instruction must align with goals and assessments (Walberg, cited in Cawelti 1995). What Walberg calls "curricular focus" means that the components of the system—goals, learning activities, and assessments—are "well matched in content and emphasis" (p. 11). The current emphasis on standards-based education—properly implemented—is a promising development (Marzano and Kendall 1996). Without clear learning standards, teachers and others in the system lack a common language and focus. Defined standards—like results—urge us to "begin with the end in mind." They define the end—those learning goals that are frequently selected and defined haphazardly (Rosenholtz 1991).

Clear, intelligible standards still elude us—a problem that the state and professional subject area documents have inadvertently exacerbated in some cases (Schmoker and Marzano 1999). At the state and local level, it is paramount that we select, and then provide a clear, simple set of standards for every teacher that corresponds richly with the assessments by which we and our communities will judge our progress. Du Four and Eaker tell the story of Henry, a high school teacher whose students were performing well below expectations. With the guidance of his principal, he began to more methodically align his instruction with the common standards set by his department. The results were worth it: Student grades improved dramatically, and Henry's students outperformed the total group on the common, comprehensive exam at the end of the semester (DuFour and Eaker 1998, pp. 190–192).

Though there is much research to be done, we are surrounded by similarly effective strategies and structures for improvement. But translating strategies into results will require changes at the systems level.

Research—and Development

Every district office must have a research and development arm—and a systematic program for ensuring its viability. Too many professional development efforts have dissipated into the "sort of" syndrome described by Robby Champion (1998, p. 7). "Sort of" staff development looks good on paper, features a nice panoply of ongoing (if untested) offerings and events, but devolves into insignificance because it is starved for results-oriented structures.

The district office must provide such structures. The district's job is to assemble a committee of practitioners who review and locate the best research for helping students to reach designated district standards. Staff development time must be devoted exclusively to proven or research-based methods that ensure student success. In Geneva (New York) City Schools, "Professional Development must prove that it matches the focus of the standards and demonstrate that it will produce results *or it is not offered*" (Richardson 1998, p. 50, emphasis added). This kind of hard-headed approach is long overdue.

The next step is to establish times on the school calendar for learning *and for follow-up*. The committee's task is to devise an efficient system for sharing and disseminating in-district results, featuring the best local implementations of research-based practices that are indexed clearly to district standards. Similarly, the district office can coordinate the collection of locally constructed, research-based lessons, units, and assessments that have enabled students to acquire challenging content and skills.

The area of research and staff development represents abundant opportunities at the district level, as many district offices are discovering (Sparks and Hirsh 1997). Why not begin collecting a set of clear, understandable core articles, representing both hard research and case studies of schools and districts that have gotten great results? What would happen if more districts—like the successful Flowing Wells District in Tucson, Arizona—built their staff development around a manageable core of research-based practices that clearly promote success within and among every subject area?

In a related way, districts and consortiums could begin sharing the results of local teacher action research on successful strategies for teaching the myriad specific and difficult concepts and standards for which—let's face it—research may not exist or is incomplete (e.g., telling time; writing a clear, arresting introduction; generating a viable hypothesis for a science investigation). We could offer small cash prizes to teacher teams for inventing strategies, as well as for "swiping" and succeeding with them.

It is time to mark the end of "sort of" staff development. Before adopting any initiative, teams should evaluate it on two levels:

1. Is it effective? Is there a convincing body of evidence that indicates a high probability of success?

2. Will there be clear, organized follow-up structures? Are there means for assessing its effect on student learning on an ongoing basis?

* * *

The key is to marry a district priority on learning to an obsession with funding and the school calendar. We must systematically exploit every opportunity for improvement by looking at (1) all district funds—especially entitlement and improvement funds—and (2) available times for teachers to learn and refine the most effective methods collaboratively. If we do this, we dramatically increase the odds of steady, incremental improvement in student learning.

5

Redefining Results

It is time for a more balanced and pragmatic understanding of "results." This redefinition should demystify what happens in schools—for teachers, parents, and students—who need more meaningful indicators of progress and clear descriptions and examples of the kinds of work we want students to be able to do. Test scores and letter grades by themselves do not give us this kind of information. The current revolution in assessment makes a new definition possible—one that includes but is not limited to standardized tests and other traditional assessments.

Beyond Standardized Scores and Dropout Rates

"Results" should take us beyond the exclusive use of such annual indicators as test scores and dropout rates. If we want these to improve (and who doesn't?), we need to focus on the short-term results and feedback that tell us how we are doing in reaching short-term subgoals and long-term goals. Such efforts give us more timely information and a more informative "report card" for the communities we serve. School report cards are still hopelessly narrow, containing little information about student achievement (Jaeger, Gorney, and Johnson 1994) and concealing more than they reveal.

"Results" too often refers to the most limited and remote kind of large-scale, annually assembled data. The problem is that such data do not inform or derive from a teacher's ongoing weekly and monthly efforts. Peters (1987) is *almost* right when he says that "what gets measured gets done" (p. 480). Things get done only if the data we gather can inform and inspire those in a position to make a difference. Information must promote purpose, and the right information must be available to practitioners when they need it.

We must be careful to measure what matters, especially what matters to those who can implement change. We need to analyze not only standardized tests, but also local, teacher-generated assessments; not only annual or summative scores, but also ongoing improvement data; not only progress toward long-term objectives, but also progress toward specific short-term or ad hoc subgoals; not only progress toward academic results, but occasionally toward student behavior goals that are linked to those results. All these should constitute the new model for assessment and results.

As we have seen, Csikszentmihalyi (1990) discovered that people will not work eagerly and imaginatively toward goals they do not regard as their own. When we judge schools solely on the basis of a few annual, one-size-fits-all measures, we risk alienating practitioners. They know that test scores and dropout rates, though important, do not tell the whole story.

Accountability—with a Human Face

We must make sure that accountability focuses primarily on improvement. The information we collect and analyze should help us to understand and improve instructional processes that help get better results. Our constituents should be informed of our work and progress so that we can all work together more effectively.

We have a ways to go. McDonald (1993) provides a telling illustration. Two parents ask how their 14-year-old is doing in middle school. This is, they discover, not a simple request. They need to consult with each of six teachers, who provide anecdotal evidence and grades—both of which can be inflated or which may reflect varying levels of accuracy. Parents want something reliable and objective. The closest thing to reliability and simplicity is standardized test scores—understanding them is easier than trying to negotiate the mysteries of the current reporting system.

By failing to supplement standardized tests with richer, more meaningful alternatives, we unwittingly invite our communities to use only test scores to judge us. We set ourselves up to be judged by an assessment that few of us believe is adequate. The upshot is this weird dance that includes everything from a constructive attempt to improve test scores to outright denial and manipulation of these scores—like we see in connection with the "Lake Wobegon effect"; all the children in every state were found to be above average. Such machinations are hardly the stuff of purposeful, passionate goal-oriented effort. Without abandoning conventional and standardized measures, we have an opportunity to break this game wide open.

Demystifying Results: The Rubrics Revolution

One of the most promising developments in assessment is the increased use of rubrics—or scoring guides—with their capacity to provide useful, quantitative data on clear, carefully selected, *qualitative* criteria. "Rubric" simply means a rule or guide. In education, it's the written criteria—or guide—by which student performance or a product is judged. Wiggins includes simple criteria lists under this term. Educators in the Pomperaug Regional School District (1996) in Middlebury/Southbury, Connecticut, rely heavily on such lists in every area and for a host of assignments. Rubrics can also refer to descriptions of quality, which are assigned a weighted numeric value in ascending or descending order. Figure 6.1 shows a rubric for assessing student writing. Notice how it clearly describes expectations and how the elements for "3" and "4" papers are similar to descriptions of good writing in general. The difference is that the rubric nails the criteria down, making them available to schools, teachers, parents, and students while providing clear direction and focus.

Scoring guides have many benefits. First, they promote good performance by clearly defining that performance and showing that such work is achievable. Second, they provide better feedback than the current system by requiring more precision and clarity about criteria for evaluating student work (O'Neil 1994). Third, they bring

---

FIGURE 6.1

Rubric/Scoring Guide for Assessing Student Writing

A "4" paper fully addresses the prompt and is written in a style appropriate to the genre assessed. It clearly shows an appropriate awareness of audience. The paper "comes alive" by incorporating mood, style, and creative expression. It is well organized, containing sufficient details, examples, descriptions, and insights to engage the reader. The paper displays a strong beginning, a fully developed middle, and an appropriate closure.

A "3" paper addresses the prompt and is written in an appropriate style. It is probably well organized and clearly written but may contain vague or inarticulate language. It shows a sense of audience but may be missing some details and examples. It has incomplete descriptions and fewer insights into characters and topics. The paper may show a weak or inappropriate beginning, middle, or ending.

A "2" paper does not fully address the prompt, which causes the paper to be rambling and disjointed. It shows little awareness of audience. The paper demonstrates an incomplete or inadequate understanding of the appropriate style. Details, facts, examples, or descriptions may be incomplete. The beginning, middle, or ending may be missing.

A "1" paper barely addresses the prompt. Awareness of audience may be missing. The paper demonstrates a lack of understanding the appropriate style. The general idea may be conveyed, but details, facts, examples, or descriptions are lacking. The beginning, middle, or ending is missing.

Source: Arizona State Assessment Program, Arizona Department of Education, Phoenix.

a welcome end to the disheartening experience we have all had: handing in an assignment without really knowing how the teacher will evaluate it and with no idea of whether the teacher will think it is excellent or shoddy.

No one wants to "fly blind." "Optimal experience" is a direct function of a "goal-directed, rule-bound action system that provides clear clues as to how well one is performing" (Csikszentmihalyi 1990, p. 71). Goals, rules, and clues are what rubrics provide by giving the kind of clarity that is essential to both enjoyment and productivity. George Hillocks (1987) found that merely using scales (another word for rubrics) was among the most significant factors that favored improved writing skills, second only to the quality and design of the writing assignment itself. If we want to maximize their impact, we should be disseminating—even displaying—rubrics everywhere: in schools, classrooms, homes—on refrigerators.

Rubrics can easily and quickly be created or adapted for any task or subject area. An excellent source for explaining how is *Assessing Student Outcomes,* by Marzano, Pickering, and McTighe (1993) and Grant Wiggins's materials in *Standards, NOT Standardization* (1993).

Promoting Learning

As Hillocks (1987) and Csikszentmihalyi (1990) have shown, people work more productively if they have clear targets. Using rubrics to establish such clarity has profound implications for educators. We all work more effectively and purposefully toward what we can see and comprehend, and the rules and clues in rubrics enable both teachers and students to understand and hence more effectively work toward higher levels of quality. The levels of achievement the rubrics represent satisfy the psychological need for progress and improvement at every level—for individuals, schools, and districts. The primary value of rubrics is their capacity to provide clear, useful feedback that can be analyzed to identify areas of strength and weakness at any time, at any level, for any number of audiences—from students to whole communities.

Promoting Purpose

Rubrics and criteria provide schools with the opportunity to begin marking improvement and identifying areas for analysis, discussion, and corrective action. We have seen how rubrics and criteria for targets such as the following can be easily developed by teams of teachers in a small amount of time:

- The number or percentage of students who can achieve proficiency levels in writing an effective position paper for social studies,

English, and science.

- The number or percentage of students who can achieve the most essential proficiencies in math, with submeasures in such areas as written demonstration, computation, and application.
- The number or percentage of students who can achieve proficiency in musical and artistic performance.
- The number or percentage of students who can achieve proficiency in oral presentations (a skill increasingly acknowledged as essential to future success).

In the Glendale Union High School District in Glendale, Arizona, students do quite well on standardized tests. But they also take rubric-scored summative assessments in almost every course. They are evaluated for their ability to write, to demonstrate scientific reasoning, and to exhibit oral presentation skills. The state has never required such tests. Glendale had the good sense to develop a system that captures and quantifies the learning that goes beyond the standardized test. With their home-grown assessment system, they can chart and analyze annual progress data for continuous improvement purposes. And they have compelling, quantitative evidence of learning that arguably subsumes and certainly goes well beyond the information provided in the standardized test.

Such an approach enables educators and communities to set the agenda together, based on a broader and richer array of indicators. Again, the good news is that rubrics are underused as part of systematic, goal-oriented improvement efforts; therefore, to the extent that we systematically implement their use, we can redefine results and move toward a better education for more students almost immediately.

Subgoals

The criteria made explicit in rubrics can themselves define the subgoals necessary to attain annual and long-term objectives. The English department at Amphitheater High School developed a common rubric for writing improvement. To promote short-term improvement, teachers focused on introductions and thesis statements as their subgoal. They devised a 3-point rubric for introductions to ensure consistency for teachers and students. The team began sharing effective strategies and materials at their regular meetings. Almost immediately, members began to see and chart improvement. Between October and December 1994, the percentage of students who were writing introductions at or above standard rose from 35 to 53 percent. By May 1995, the number increased to 82 percent. That is breakthrough improvement.

Assessing Subject-Area Content

Rubrics can be especially useful for assessing content mastery, and many are available for this type of assessment (see Marzano, Pickering, and McTighe 1993, pp. 94–95). They encourage what is perhaps the best way of demonstrating such mastery: the essay exam, which can be rubric scored. Essays not only allow students to show knowledge of large amounts of content but also emphasize the *meaning of subject knowledge*, which favors retention. The essay exam should be a part of every teacher's arsenal for teaching and assessing content. Richard Stiggins (1994), an advocate of assessing content knowledge as well as processes and skills, speaks of the "vast untapped potential" of essay assessment (p. 134). As many early 20th century exams reveal, essays assess mastery the old-fashioned way: They promote the critical, higher-order processing of content as they assess mastery of information. Rubrics can help teachers assess such work.

Of course, objective test data serve a vital (and time-efficient) function, too; grades and scores can provide data that we use to derive better, more engaging and effective ways of helping students master material. Objective test results can reveal important information:

- Concepts or content areas that students are having difficulty mastering.
- Knowledge that students don't find arresting or relevant and hence don't retain.
- The need to connect content to life or to a meaningful context.
- The need for review, discussion, or clarification.

Once we establish common goals, we should be able to conduct item analyses that reveal

- The number of students achieving at or above standard (e.g., above a certain percentage) on tests and quizzes.
- The areas of highest and lowest retention of content.

The stage is then set for substantive teacher collaboration, sharing, and brainstorming for more active and engaging ways to teach content and to creatively use or supplement a textbook. Ironically, discussing and analyzing objective test scores can lead us out of some ponderous and unengaging practices.

Success from Rubrics

States that use rubrics to assess writing have realized profound improvements. In Maryland, writing rubrics are the heart of a more general improvement effort. The rubrics are sent home to parents and posted in schools and classrooms. Teachers use and adapt them for all disciplines. The result? Over the last decade, Maryland has seen the percentage of students who reach proficiency levels rise from below 47 to above 90 percent, with breakthrough improvements occurring after only one year.

Teachers in the Oak Harbor School District in Washington had an incomplete picture of how well their students were writing. Then they developed a districtwide scoring rubric, which immediately identified deficiencies in every category. The data enabled them to begin systematically addressing the deficiencies. After one year, an outside assessor reported that "remarkable improvements" had occurred and that the new program was a "phenomenal success." The following year those gains were "sustained and improved" (Daniel 1993, p. 44).

In Colorado's Weld County School District 6, the percentage of students who learned to write at or above standard on the district writing rubric rose dramatically after the rubric was introduced during the 1988–89 school year (see Figure 3.1 on p. 36). Rubrics defined these standards and thus motivated students from all backgrounds to achieve them (Waters, Burger, and Burger 1995). Under such conditions, what gets measured (and clearly defined) does get done.

Rubrics are becoming increasingly available in all disciplines. But despite some encouraging momentum and growing awareness, teachers do not routinely use them in classrooms. Most districts don't routinely collect and analyze writing or other rubric-based performance data. This absence points up yet another huge opportunity. Rubrics may be the catalyst for generating the kind of frequent, focused, measurable improvement and performance data that effectively address professional priorities, as well as the need for accountability.

Demystifying Results with Examples of Excellence

Not all parents and children know what quality work looks like or understand the criteria for it, because few schools provide representative, intelligible examples of what they expect students to strive for (Wiggins 1994b). Parents not only want better information about what their children are learning, they want *more of it* (Jaeger, Gorney, and Johnson 1994). We have underestimated this interest. As our economy becomes increasingly knowledge based, look for this attention to increase.

The emerging interest in exemplary student work or "anchor papers" is especially fortunate. Such examples of excellence clearly exhibit what we want from students. Models and exemplary samples of student work are themselves goals: the clear, concrete expression of the results we wish children to achieve. When accompanied by descriptive rubrics, exemplary student work defines—and promotes—improvement.

We should begin displaying, publishing, and referring to models of achievement within and between every area of study. Wiggins (1994a) thinks that posting models or exemplars in schools creates an atmosphere that promotes improvement almost by itself, without administrative coercion. Seeing what children have actually done extends our sense of students' true capabilities.

A Historic Convergence

We are witnessing a historic convergence of developments: We are creating, using, and disseminating rubrics and alternative assessments more; parents want more and better information; and we are beginning to recognize that anchor papers and models make desired results less abstract and thus accelerate the ability to learn.

Norm-referenced, standardized scores have their role, but if we take advantage of the moment, the revolution now occurring will add a new dimension to assessment and reporting. Technology is an emerging partner; we may soon be able to collect, manage, and aggregate data on hand-held computers, which can quickly organize the data to reveal strengths and weaknesses on the skills and proficiencies we choose.

Rubrics are key pieces of this change in assessment, allowing us to redefine what counts in schools. Without compromising the qualitative nature of student performance, rubrics enrich and validate quantitative results, even in areas we once thought unmeasurable. No measurement is ever perfect, but rubrics allow us to evaluate more precisely and accurately areas where quality standards have traditionally been ill-defined. Rubrics represent a shift in thinking about how well or reliably we can gauge and assess such intangibles as quality writing, thought, and application. And because they promote the clarity and collective focus that research tells us is essential to improvement, they inevitably favor better results (Rosenholtz 1989, Little 1990).

Are Standardized Tests the Enemy?

The objective emphasis of standardized tests does not have to drive schools toward "drill and kill." Research shows that students who attend schools where subject matter is made relevant and interesting are retaining more and will therefore earn higher scores on standardized tests. This finding indicates that these tests are indeed useful, especially when we consider the evidence that an abundance of reading, writing, and authentic math experiences is quite possibly the best way to promote success on these tests (Krashen 1993, Resnick et al. 1991). Standardized tests can reveal both progress and areas needing improvement. Without derailing alternative efforts to gauge student performances and higher-order skills, standardized tests can help us make comparative assessments on how well our students are learning basic knowledge and skills. Such tests have been found to be an impressive predictor of future student success. Their statistical reliability is well documented (Walberg, Haertel, and Gerlach-Downie 1994).

Because standardized tests are easy to administer and routinely used, they provide a good "first level of analysis" for people wishing to improve their schools (Bamburg and Medina 1993, p. 36). In a balanced treatment of such tests' worth, Bamburg and Medina found that when used properly, tests can provide the initial leverage for improvement:

> At the school level, the disaggregation [of standardized test data] refocused the staff's purpose, reaffirmed their beliefs, increased the congruence between what was espoused and practiced, focused the instructional conversation, established data-driven priorities, and helped staff affirm that they do make a difference for all children (p. 38).

Using these tests, people such as Effective Schools consultant Larry Lezotte have helped numerous schools see and then address inequities in the quality of education they provide (Bullard and Taylor 1993).

Rubrics and Traditional Assessments: The Best of Both

Schools known for their relevant and enlightened learning activities have also realized exceptional improvement on standardized tests. It is hard to find a school where children are receiving a quality education but where standardized test scores are low.

• Teachers at Westwood School in Dalton, Georgia, undertook to depart from the restraints of a test-driven curriculum. They started with mathematics, refashioning the curriculum and orchestrating an improvement effort that would ensure greater depth, engagement, and application. After one school year, the spring achievement scores were *the highest to date* (Livingston, Castle, and Nations 1989). Their experience is not unique.

• In an inner-city setting, Resnick and her associates set out to improve student math performance, using "as little school drill material as possible" to teach math with manipulatives and other rich, "reasoning-based" methods. In one year, 1st grade math scores rose from a mean of about the 25th to the 80th percentile. The following year, mean achievement with the experimental group was at the 70th percentile (Resnick et al. 1991, p. 47).

•   The Junior Great Books (JGB) program has a long and celebrated reputation for helping students to read and critically assess quality literature through close reading and discussion—what they call "shared inquiry." Until recently, JGB was just "another staff development program without supporting evidence." Now it has acquired "a strong and diverse body of evidence" that includes significant measurable improvement on several state, norm-referenced and cognitive/critical thinking tests (Criscuola 1998, p. 14).

•   The Coalition of Essential Schools' Central Park East Secondary School in East Harlem, New York, saw gains in test scores when former Director Deborah Meier and her new faculty came in with a philosophy that emphasized interactive teaching methods and learning activities: writing workshops, thematic units, discussion, and inquiry (Schmoker and Wilson 1993).

•   According to Stan Pogrow, "The biggest secret in American education is that at-risk students love to learn and be challenged with very sophisticated tasks" (1990, p. 62). Pogrow's Higher-Order Thinking Skills (HOTS) program, emphasizing complex tasks and Socratic questioning and thinking skills, has helped numerous schools get better results on standardized tests in both reading and math (1988, 1990). At 2,000 school sites in 48 states, the HOTS program has realized, on average, twice the gains of alternative approaches used at those same schools; the program has had three times the gains in reading comprehension. Using this carefully researched, metacognitive approach, 5th graders throughout the Detroit Public Schools gained 16 months in reading and 13 months in math during the 1994–95 school year. Recent implementation at Elvira Elementary School in Tucson, Arizona, was successful by several measures. In one year, standardized scores in reading and math went up 13.5 normal curve equivalents (NCEs), as did writing scores and GPAs, irrespective of socioeconomic status.

Standardized tests, if disaggregated and thoughtfully analyzed, can provide feedback and goal-orientation. By themselves, the tests haven't universally inspired teachers to reach viable goals. They don't sufficiently or frequently enough capture the kind of education we should provide. Unless supplemented by other richer and more precise indicators, they have a limited and possibly an unfortunate influence on instruction and its improvement (Smith 1991; Haladyna, Nolen, and Haas 1991).

The real problem, as Wiggins points out, "is not [standardized] tests per se but the failure of classroom teachers...to be results focused and data driven"—to use these results wisely and as part of a wider array of assessments (Wiggins 1994a, pp. 17–18).

Another problem is our failure to report on the results achieved with other assessments—like increased rates of success on literary and social studies essays, science performances, and multistep, open-ended math problems. Why not report these? Why not begin making them a part of the public conversation? Schools must take the initiative here.

We must now move toward a new accountability, a new results-orientation, analogous to the baseball card that Wiggins (1994b) uses to illustrate how we should begin marking progress for ourselves, parents, and communities. Win-loss records (like standard grades) are one thing; a baseball card contains *a variety* of significant, specific results, such as stolen bases, batting averages, runs batted in, walks, and strikeouts. Educationally analogous information should be the new norm for education. Like Wiggins's baseball card, the information we gather should enable us to chart and disseminate a richer variety of results. We can thus proclaim the legitimacy of school or district assessments that measure student performance in many areas:

- Musical and artistic performances.
- Quarterly or semester content essay exams.
- Discussion and listening skills.
- Debate and oral presentation skills.
- Student behavior and responsibility.
- Ability to solve multistep math problems and apply math principles.
- Ability to write effective analytical or persuasive papers in social studies and literature.
- Ability to conduct and write up a scientific experiment.

Redesigning Report Cards

If we truly wish to change the way we assess, the report card may be one of the main leverage points. The Key School in Indianapolis provides progress reports for each of Howard Gardner's seven areas of intelligence. The Kyrene School District in Tempe, Arizona, reports student levels of development in three activities not typically assessed on report cards:

- Reads fluently.
- Makes sensible predictions.
- Uses word recognition strategies (i.e., phonics structure and context).

As a parent, I'd *love* to get such information on my daughters' progress. The Tucson Unified School District piloted a similar report card in 25 schools, which provides rubrics for everything from the traditional content areas to student progress in learning to become a "collaborative worker" and a "self-directed learner." Parents, predictably enough, gave the report card good reviews (Clarridge and Whitaker 1994).

For Bob Marzano and John Kendall, a radically different report card—and grade book—are in order: one that reveals strengths and weaknesses relative to specific, carefully designated standards (1996, pp. 125–172). This new report card is being piloted in several school districts.

Bena Kallick (personal communication 1999) points out that we must not expect to jump from traditional assessments to the exclusive use of alternative assessments overnight. Of course, she's right. The key is to exploit the many opportunities we currently have for improvement within the current framework, while earning the additional opportunities that will come with improvement and success.

The next chapter will explore some of those available opportunities in more detail.

7

Opportunities for Action Within and Among the Subject Areas

This chapter suggests options and opportunities for beginning the venture toward results-oriented improvement. While they are not intended to be prescriptive, the options are offered in the confidence that any school or district can implement something similar. The process can be accelerated if we begin to systematically bank and disseminate the best assessments in our schools, districts, and states. Optimally, such assessments must be conducted and analyzed not just annually but regularly during the school year.

The discussion assumes that despite the obvious state of ferment in curriculum and assessment, we do not have to succumb to paralysis. We can do much to embrace the best of the past and anticipate and prepare ourselves for the future. We can organize for results now—and we can get them.

The Subject Areas

The current interest in interdisciplinary learning still leaves room for emphasizing the disciplines. As Howard Gardner points out, we must not be in a rush to toss out the disciplinary baby with the bath water; a good grounding in the disciplines is the best basis for interdisciplinary success (Gardner and Boix-Mansilla 1994). Even those who advocate integrating the disciplines have cautioned that for practical reasons, we need to begin with strategies that embrace, rather than diminish, the legitimacy of the disciplines (Ackerman 1989; Marzano and Kendall 1996). Frederick County, Maryland, Director of Assessment Steve Hess, who helped found the Maryland Assessment Consortium, recommends that strongly emphasizing application *within* the content areas is the best grounding for authentic integration within and *among* the disciplines. Striking the right balance takes time; we are still finding our way on this journey. In the meantime, consider some possibilities for action that we can take now in specific subject areas.

Social Studies

Educator Walter Parker (1991) believes that social studies is in a state of relative disarray. Grades and credits reflect nothing more than time spent in class and "practically nothing about the abilities and understanding that graduates have or have not achieved" (p. 15). As an antidote, he recommends building a social studies curriculum around benchmark assessments. Sample assessments from Parker and the National History Standards Project are shown in Figure 7.1. As you examine them, consider how easily they can be adapted and administered. Consider, too, how powerfully they can orient social studies teaching toward attaining both content mastery and higher-order intellectual achievement. Teachers can generate assessments like these for every unit of social studies, from history to current issues and events. Discussion and activities can then reinforce and prepare students to succeed on such assessments.

FIGURE 7.1
Sample Benchmark Assessments for a Social Studies Curriculum

At the End of Elementary School
Students write a summary of a current public controversy drawn from school life and tell how a courageous and civic-minded American they have studied (e.g., Sojourner Truth or James Madison) might decide to act on the issue.

At the End of Junior High/Middle School
Students write an analysis of a current public controversy facing their community and draw an historical comparison.

Source: Parker 1991, pp. 24–25.

* * *

Grades 7–12
Analyze the connection between political ideas and economic interests [for a certain nation(s) or historical period(s)] and compare the ideas and interests of different groups.

Source: National History Standards Project.

The Pomperaug Regional School District in Middlebury, Connecticut, has used questions based on topics that the Bradley Commission and the National Geographic Society outlined. Such comprehensive but manageable criteria have generated both wonderful assessments and essential questions for a social studies curriculum. For example, teachers use the following questions for a unit on culture:

- **Grades 5 and 6.** "How does the specific geography and environment influence the development of that culture?"
- **Grades 7 and 8.** "What values, beliefs, political ideas, and institutions have the people of the United States developed?"
- **Grade 11.** "How have geographic factors contributed to the development of regions of the United States? How did these differences fuel the Civil War?"

The 1999 New York Regents exam includes sample questions like this for Global History:

> Define the term "nationalism." Then select one nation you have studied and give specific historical examples of nationalism within that country. Describe a situation where nationalism was either a positive or a negative force in that country's history (New York State 1998).

Such open-ended, "essential questions" or learning tasks invite elaborated, interpretive responses that get at content in a meaningful and arresting way. The Australian graduation exams contain similar questions, *without* raising hackles about national versus local preference and control. Such questions allow considerable teacher and student autonomy within a common framework known as the "Common Assessment Tasks." The Australian assessments demonstrate that even national assessments don't necessarily stifle local influence. It *can* be done (Howe and Vickers 1993). Orienting social studies toward such questions promotes a thoughtful, engaging, inquiry-driven treatment of knowledge and content and increases the possibilities for interdisciplinary tie-ins to science and language arts. It all starts with high-quality questions.

Any number of rubrics can be used to evaluate responses to such prompts, including modifying the rubrics we discussed in Chapter 6. A rubric from Marzano, Pickering, and McTighe's book (1993), which is full of excellent rubrics and representative learning activities, is a good example of one that can be adapted for social studies. Figure 7.2 (on p. 92) shows Level 4 of the rubric.

Short-term subgoals can be developed from part or all of an assessment. For example, teachers can collect and analyze the con-

FIGURE 7.2
Level 4 of a 4-Point Rubric for Written Assignments

A. Effectively interprets and synthesizes information
   4: Consistently interprets the information gathered for tasks in accurate and highly insightful ways and provides unique syntheses of that information.

Source: Marzano, Pickering, and McTighe 1993, p. 96.

crete components of "insightful" responses, then share strategies for improving student capacity for such insights. Teams can then collect data on the number of students satisfying the criteria or achieving at a "3" or "4" level—and then determine which will be the most germane interventions for increasing that number.

Results and continuous improvement in the social studies can be relatively simple. Teachers can regularly collaborate to compare, either in general or numerical terms, how students are doing on conventional objective tests and quizzes or on essay exams. Sharing lessons and methods promotes higher scores; sharing unit assessments saves time and promotes a broader, more precise collaboration. As Rosenholtz points out, similarity of goals enables professionals to more capably help each other.

Language Arts and Literature

In the preceding chapters, we examined several cases of improvement in the language arts, specifically in writing. Although all disciplines should stress good written and oral communication, the language arts play an important general role: cultivating the communications skills that are vital to every discipline. But English and language arts have their own domains as well: literature and its understanding. A full education must provide opportunities to ponder, explore, discuss, and analyze the richness of human experience, which novels, poetry, short stories, and poetry afford. In social studies, students can debate the wisdom of the United States entering World War I; in language arts, they can read and discuss the deeper human issues raised in *All Quiet on the Western Front*.

As students begin to read literature insightfully, we can use rubrics to gauge their development. Again, a good source for such rubrics is found in *Assessing Student Outcomes,* by Marzano, Pickering, and McTighe (1993). When we can assess the growth of students' critical reading skills relative to documents like the U.S. Constitution,

FIGURE 7.3
Level 4 of a 4-Point Rubric for Math

Goal: Every student will be able to effectively solve math problems.
  Possible subgoals: Every student will be able to produce solutions that
  • Show complete understanding of the problem.
  • Thoroughly address all points relevant to the solution.
  • Show logical reasoning and valid conclusions.
  • Communicate effectively and clearly through writing and/or diagrams.
  • Include adequate and correct computations and/or setup.

Source: Adapted from the Arizona State Assessment Program, Arizona Department of Education, Phoenix.

The Diary of Anne Frank, or an editorial on the effects of acid rain, we open the door to meaningful, focused collaboration among teachers.

Another good measurement is the number of books students read, which research shows is among the best indicators of student reading development. Stephen Krashen's studies (1993) found that creating conditions conducive to lots of reading promotes everything from vocabulary development to comprehension and writing skills (and higher test scores).

Math

Earlier chapters described how teachers can get better results on conventional tests by developing and administering common assessments together. Math teachers can apply this principle by quickly scanning test results for strengths and weaknesses and then discussing better ways to teach to the areas of weakness. Such constructive, targeted collaboration may begin with research-based minilessons that address the most apparent priorities revealed by the study.

Math teachers can collaborate to get better results in higher-order math proficiencies as well. For instance, when teachers are working from the same math rubric, their conversation can revolve around the common elements and criteria described in that rubric. Figure 7.3 shows Level 4 of a rubric that can be used to assess content, computation, and higher-order mathematical processes. At regular intervals, teachers can discuss student success—or frustration—on any part of the rubric. A well-organized team can go one step further by charting collective progress on the same assessment at certain intervals to even more precisely observe trends in improvement.

Obviously, mathematics *is* evolving. How do we keep pace with the changes? Consider the National Council of Teachers of Mathematics' (NCTM) statement on algebra, *Algebra for Everyone* (National Council of Teachers of Mathematics 1994). NCTM regrets the current state of teaching algebra "divorced from any natural context" (p. 1). They are calling for a shift from algebra as a set of manipulative skills to algebra as a means of representation. That shift requires that we do more to stress quantitative patterns and relationships as they appear in statistics, shape, and change. All we have to do is add such problems and components to both instruction and assessment. In some cases, we may need to substitute one problem for another on formative or summative assessments, substituting a multistep or application problem for one that only requires computation. In others, we may need to add a component to an already existing problem—for example, a requirement to provide a written explanation for how to solve the problem. Either way, we can progress, adjust, and meet the future without having to wait indefinitely until the state of the discipline fully settles—which will never happen. We always need to maintain a balance of computation, application, and representation in mathematics.

Science

Science, too, is in a state of ferment. Like math, science has an excessive amount of content to cover, about two to three times as much as in other countries (U.S. Department of Education 1998). But while we wait for the needed paring of the science curriculum, we can begin getting better results now on both objective tests and alternative assessments and performances.

Shavelson and Baxter (1992) write that "a combination of indicators (e.g., multiple-choice and performance assessments) may be needed to provide a complete picture of achievement" (p. 23). In addition to objective tests, they recommend such time-efficient assessments as "notebook surrogates," in which students describe a scientific investigation so clearly and logically that a friend can then repeat the same steps accurately. Shavelson and Baxter contend that such methods are inexpensive and fairly easy to assess—about one to two minutes per student. If these notebooks are rubric scored, we will have progressive, numerical data to mark improvement and use as a base for instructional adjustments throughout the school year.

More elaborate assessments can occur regularly but less frequently. Sizer (1992) provides a good example of the kind of science assessment that can be periodically administered to determine how well students' scientific knowledge is transferring to more lifelike contexts. Students are asked to act as nutritionists to design and defend three menus. Each menu must meet the following criteria:

- Stay within a budget of $2.56 per serving.
- Meet the requirements for maximum nutrition.
- Be attractive to students.

Even occasional assessments such as these supplement—and inform—the traditional science curriculum, which all the science foundations are unanimous in telling us are too long on content and short on application.

K–12 teachers in Lake Havasu, Arizona, met for one week in the summer of 1997 to create district criterion-referenced tests for science for each grade level. Their process was a fairly simple one:

1. Review the (invariably too-numerous) science standards.
2. Select only the most essential topics to focus on and assess.
3. Develop both objective test items and performance assessments for the respective topics.

Most of the work was completed that week. For the first time, district teachers had a common curricular focus and hence an opportunity for richer, more meaningful collaboration.

Educators in Connecticut's Pomperaug Regional School District (1966) assign students designated tasks at the primary, elementary, and upper elementary levels. At each level, tasks fall in four major categories: (1) "Scientific Process," (2) "Graphs and Related Products," (3) "Science Products," and (4) "Communication Products Using Science Content." Each category has 6 to 10 common performance tasks for students to complete; each task has assessments and criteria.

Most schools are not this organized. But teachers at any grade or level can get started by selecting areas of strong emphasis or agreement in the science curriculum, developing one or more assessment tasks for those areas, and building from there. One simple approach is to modify an activity that most teachers already do. Eventually, common tasks and assessments—even content mastery tests—can be developed for each quarter or semester and the results gathered and analyzed.

Such an effort can begin with one common test or performance task evaluated with the same criteria. Teachers can then compile the collective results anonymously to see how their own students compare to the group standard. This comparison immediately creates the opportunity to examine the most exemplary student work using common assessment criteria. Once teachers feel comfortable with the first step, they can select another task or a comprehensive or end-of-term assessment. Teachers have autonomy while they move carefully toward a reasonable level of consensus on what they want students to learn about science. As such efforts begin to pull teachers and their collective brainpower together, the benefits for students will be enormous.

Frequent, Collective Assessment—Not as Daunting as It Seems

Regular, collective assessment isn't as difficult as it may at first seem. It is as easy as (1) getting a team of teachers together to review year-end state or district summative tests, or the skills the teachers will measure that year, and (2) selecting or developing a small but representative handful of problems to develop short-term assessments and subgoals. One each quarter—or even each semester—can get the process started.

That's what Dan Hendery and his math team at Johnson City High School did. And they got remarkable results. They created a battery of assessments by reviewing past copies of the New York Regents exam. They quickly selected about 25 representative problems for each exam and administered them quarterly. After each assessment, they conducted an item analysis—together—in which they discussed problems or areas where students were notably strong or struggling. The result? The first year, the percentage of students succeeding on the Regents exam rose from 47 to 93 percent. They now use this approach to promote success in math at the elementary level as well. Such a simple, quarterly strategy allows both teachers and students to head off failure before the end of the year, when it is too late to help. These exams have been easy to use and update yearly. Teachers can swap problems as the summative exams evolve or add multistep problems and alternative assessments as emphases shift.

A team from one of our schools, Holaway Elementary, realized continuous improvement as members gathered data using a 3-part rubric they created for math. Part 1 measured student performance in computation; Part 2, logical reasoning (as seen through student writing); and Part 3, demonstration (skillful and appropriate use of equations). At regularly scheduled meetings lasting about 30 minutes, they analyzed the data on just one multistep problem (a great way for any team to get started) to see what was working and which areas most needed shoring up. Then they brainstormed for solutions to problems the data revealed. In each of the three areas, they saw steady improvement; Figure 7.4 shows how students improved in logical reasoning.

Improvement like this is doable. We don't need to wait until a full-blown battery of assessments is firmly established in every state or district—which themselves are always subject to change (as it should be). We must begin where we are and move forward immediately by starting small and capitalizing on what's at hand.

Educators in Connecticut's Pomperaug Regional School District (1996) have developed one of the most sophisticated and impressive

FIGURE 7.4

Percentage of Students Achieving Level 3 or Higher on Logical
Reasoning, One of Three Areas Measured in a Math Rubric*

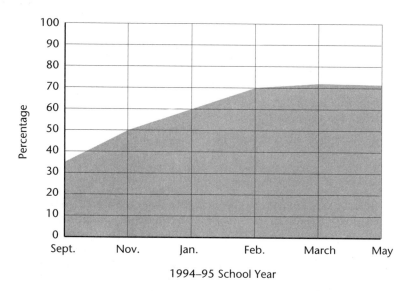

1994–95 School Year

*The 4-point rubric measures performance in computation, logical reasoning, and
demonstration.*
Source: Holaway Elementary School, Tucson, Arizona.

alternative assessment programs in the United States. Even so, administrators urge teachers to start small as they move into the world
of performance assessment, to select a project that they "already
assign to their students," and to "make this task a short, simple, and
easy one." Assistant Superintendent Michael Hibbard recommends
starting with a team or department that is willing to experiment with
one performance assessment. The aim is to promote immediate but
ongoing, incremental improvement.

Ted Sizer's book, *Horace's School: Redesigning the American High
School* (1992), is punctuated with suggested exhibitions that can serve
as excellent benchmark assessments for data-driven, throughout-the-
year improvements. For example, one exhibition asks students to
decide whether they should buy a 1988 Ford Tempo or a 1988 Toyota
Corolla. They are required to address the following concerns:

- Mileage
- Price of the car and cost of insurance

- Impact of the cost over four years relative to earnings
- Impact relative to entertainment budget

Such problems and assessments can easily be matched or tailored for quarterly or end-of-unit assessments. Teams of teachers offering the same course can set these types of subgoals at department meetings or special sessions, then analyze the results.

Let's look at how some of the better report cards can provide opportunities for data-based improvement. As we've seen, new report cards are creating opportunities for data-based improvement in school districts throughout the United States. For example, on its report cards, the Kyrene School District lists indicators to monitor student success in math:

- Counts to 50/100/Beyond 100.
- Skip-counts by 10's/5's/2's.
- Uses strategies to solve problem situations.
- Makes and reads simple graphs.

Teachers can monitor aggregate data on grade-level and school-wide student success in these areas, either generally or within a more data-driven scheme. Analyzing data and developing strategies on how to promote collective progress (e.g., the number or percentage of students who are mastering each task and the best ways to improve that number) create opportunities to achieve short-term, break-through results. These results can be prominently charted, showing the incremental impact of faculty collaboration and adjustment to instruction as teachers strive to help greater numbers of students.

Knowing Where They Stand

In any subject area, students and teachers want to know where they stand in relation to achievable standards. When we work to improve—at anything—knowing how well we're doing is essential. An increasing amount of evidence indicates that providing this information helps students. As we have seen, Colorado's Weld County School District has had great success by carefully monitoring both individual and aggregate student progress in writing, reading, and math, using a continuous improvement model. Teachers take great pains to ensure that all students have truly reached requisite levels of achievement before moving on—a fairly radical departure from what happens in the average school (Waters, Burger, and Burger 1995).

Results Among the Disciplines

Some results span the disciplines. The first three discussed here are gaining momentum: the ability to make oral presentations, to participate effectively in discussions, and to read critically and interpretively. They may seem to have their home in the language arts. But they are increasingly being seen as important elements of a quality education in every subject area.

The Oral Presentation

Like writing, making effective presentations has implications for every discipline. The ability to orally present, propose, and persuade is a key skill and can provide intrinsic motivation for students to find purpose in their studies. Learning, without any opportunities to share what we've learned, is a little like cooking for ourselves; we do it, but we probably won't do it as well. One of the most exciting and energized classrooms I have ever seen was a high school business and careers class taught by Dolores Christensen at Gilbert High School in Gilbert, Arizona. I was amazed to learn that only students who were two or more years behind in their core courses were eligible for the course. When I asked Dolores what the secret for such enthusiastic activity was, she said, without hesitating, that the weekly oral presentations the students had to do lent immediacy and purpose to their research.

The Key School in downtown Indianapolis had the prescience to make the oral presentation the cornerstone of their assessment program. A videotape of several student presentations per year follows students throughout their school career.

Baltimore's Walbrook High School, a member of the Coalition of Essential Schools, has made the oral presentation a key exhibition for students to demonstrate mastery for high school graduation.

At Amphitheater High School, a team of English and social studies teachers developed a rubric to evaluate student oral presentations. Part of the rubric evaluated students' introductions to their presentations, using the following criteria:

- Arouses interest.
- Is appropriate to the topic.
- Is brief and to the point.

Though the main goal is to measurably improve the quality of oral presentations, an excellent subgoal that teachers pursued for a period was better introductions (which their data revealed was an area where students seemed to have the most difficulty). This subgoal approach resulted in an increasingly higher percentage of students making quality oral presentations "at or above standard" during the 1994-95 school year: from 32 percent in October, to 58 percent in December, to 64 percent in March.

Walbrook High School in Baltimore used this same focused, analytical approach to achieve documented improvement in the quality of student presentations. Notice how improvement in any of the following areas can constitute a subgoal. But notice as well how rich yet common-sensical they are. By collaboratively viewing and discussing student presentations, Walbrook teachers decided to take the following improvement actions:

- Schedule oral presentations earlier in the year.
- Do more to suggest topics to students within areas of interest.
- Ask students to do a trial run and refine it during their junior year for their senior year presentation.
- Make the criteria for evaluation more specific (Turner and Finney 1993).

The team at Amphitheater High School came up with the following suggestions after one collaborative session:

- Hand out rubrics in advance of all assignments.
- Show and analyze the best model presentations on videotape.
- Make sure students practice more frequently but for smaller groups rather than for the entire class.
- Help students concentrate on and rehearse introductions, an area of major difficulty.

The insights contained in the preceding lists show that collaboration allows teachers to capture each other's fund of collective intelligence. A clear goal optimizes the quality of their sharing; they are organized to succeed. In the isolation and crush of events that is a teacher's life, time to evaluate and refocus is limited. The list from Amphitheater High School is from a longer list of 23 suggestions for improvement generated by the team—in 15 minutes. Some of the teachers said that they learned more from each other in that 15 minutes than at any other time. Their effort paid off, for them and for the students, who expressed a high level of satisfaction at having the opportunity to sharpen their speaking skills.

Improving Discussion Skills

Let's look at another related area for results—discussion. Documents such as the U.S. Department of Labor's SCANS report (Secretary's Commission on Achieving Necessary Skills 1992) tell us that the ability to speak, listen, and interact intelligently is emerging as one of the pivotal proficiencies in the workplace of the future. Other research supports this conclusion:

> In the economy of the 21st century, all indications are that speaking and listening will be among the most important skills (Daggett 1994, pp. 20–21).

Substantive discussions are also among the best settings to exercise and enlarge one's intellectual and reasoning capacities:

> Discussion is the most basic and essential form of participatory citizenship. It is in discussion that disagreements are revealed, clarified, and analyzed; alternatives created and explored... common purposes perceived; decisions made; action planned. Talk is not cheap (Parker 1991, p. vi).

Unfortunately, discussion has been relegated to the periphery of skills and activities that make up the school day. Nonetheless, the Coalition of Essential Schools, as well as the Paideia Program, have seen it as being at the very heart of an education. The Paideia Program goes so far as to recommend that about a third of a student's school time be spent examining and analyzing ideas in discussion (Adler 1982). Research conducted in Amphitheater reveals that students count discussion among their favorite and most stimulating school activities. (The Junior Great Books Foundation provides excellent training in conducting guided discussions.)

Peter Cookson's (1985) study of the best private schools in the United States has similarly profound implications. It reveals that regular participation in discussions is one of the most distinguishing features of these institutions. The recurring opportunity to articulate and interpret ideas gives their graduates a decided advantage in making their way in the world.

Most school discussions are restricted to recall, parroting material just read. According to Gamoran and Nystrand (1992), an average student's school week includes *little or no discussion* that invites students to interpret and express ideas and opinions. This is regrettable. We should begin to see dialogue as one of the most engaging, intellectually enlarging activities we have for promoting the listening and critical thinking skills that students need so badly. It is at the heart of democratic participation, equipping a citizenry for the responsibility of self-government.

Discussion is a skill we should assess, especially in the early grades, when some students are likely to get left behind their more assertive classmates. Assessment helps ensure that all students have the opportunity to acquire a facility with discussion. Stiggins (1994) describes a process that he calls "scored discussions"; students can produce criteria such as the following to evaluate the discussions:

- Listening attentively when others are contributing.
- Asking clarifying questions.
- Making points clear and brief.
- Being confident to take a position and defend it.

Such criteria can serve as subgoals and be developed into a discussion rubric. One way to assess a discussion is for students to assemble themselves into two circles, one inside the other. The group in the inner circle discusses, while the group on the periphery documents and tallies data on the frequency and quality of the contributions that the inside group makes. Subgoals can include trying to reach an ever-higher number of students, quarterly or monthly, who are improving in a specific subskill (e.g., making points clear and brief) or who can perform at or above standard (e.g., satisfying the criteria or earning a "3" or "4" on a 4-point discussion rubric).

Reading

Reading is another area that spans the disciplines. In the lower grades, reading means acquiring the basic skills of decoding and comprehension. After students learn the basics of construing text, they need to learn the art of mining a text for meaning. As my friend Wayne Dotts likes to say, they pass from "learning to read" to "reading to learn."

Learning to Read. Rapid advances are occurring in our ability to teach reading, especially in our ability to monitor progress and adjust teaching practice. The success of programs such as Reading Recovery, Success for All, and Reading Renaissance is built on the notion we have been stressing:

> Successful early-intervention programs include systematic regular assessment in order to monitor progress and provide a basis for instructional planning (Pikulski 1994, p. 37).

The Success for All program has succeeded in a large proportion of the schools where it has been used (Slavin et al. 1994). One cornerstone practice is giving quarterly tests, which provide information for the express purpose of informing and adjusting instruction to get better results.

As we have seen (Chapter 3) schools can easily monitor and celebrate periodic increases in the number of students reaching established thresholds of proficiency (e.g., above 90 percent on a running-record assessment) each month or grading period. Again, collecting and charting these data—anonymously—by school or grade level takes no more than a few minutes for everyone involved.

In addition to giving tests for improving results, another ongoing goal (or subgoal) can be to increase the number of lower-achieving students who graduate out of the remedial pullout component in the programs—who reach reading levels where they no longer need individual tutoring sessions to keep up with their peers.

Many successful intervention programs include similar indicators, which teachers use to gauge student progress:

- Ability to recognize prescribed sight words.
- Ability to identify all lowercase and uppercase letters.
- Ability to recognize phonemic cues and consonant blends.

These, too, are emerging on report cards, providing focus for teachers and richer information for parents, thus creating clear goals for all to work toward. The 1st grade report card for the Ann Arbor Public Schools includes the following indicators:

- Reads fluently at his or her reading level.
- Demonstrates knowledge of story structure.
- Identifies the topic and two or more supporting details of an informational book read to students.

Teachers can monitor the pace at which groups of children work, from "not yet" to "developing," to "achieving" in these areas. The data can be used to identify areas of primary concern from quarter to quarter and help teachers reach year-end reading proficiency goals.

Even monitoring the number of vocabulary words students master can correlate to reading ability. Interestingly, the number of vocabulary words students learn—through direct instruction—can have a powerful impact on reading ability (Marzano and Marzano 1988). Using a program called *Jump Start*, a teacher in the Denver Public Schools used a combination of direct instruction and games to teach students approximately 500 words during a summer school session. After only 18 two-hour sessions, his students averaged a seven and a half month gain on a standardized reading test. As Marzano and others point out, to learn vocabulary is to learn concepts—which enlarges learning capacity.

Reading to Learn. The potential for student benefit is enormous in this area. Consider the manifold applications of the goal shown in Figure 7.5 (on p. 104), adapted from a state-level reading rubric. The goal merges reading and writing: Students write to reveal their skill as thoughtful, perceptive readers. Again, as helpful as such criteria may be for focusing and identifying short-term subgoals, there is no substitute for models and anchor papers that reveal student ability to express sound interpretation in writing. Abundant opportunities exist within and among every discipline for students to produce written evidence of careful, perceptive reading. Offering students the opportunity to examine exemplary pieces not only adds flesh to the descriptions and criteria but also provides a nonthreatening guide and guards against gross variations in standards.

FIGURE 7.5
Goal and Subgoals for Reading

Goal: All students can demonstrate a complex understanding and interpreta-
tion of a text.
   Subgoals: All students will demonstrate
- Considerable evidence of extension of the text (connection to other texts, experiences, and generalizations).
- Evidence of "reading like a writer": evaluating and appreciating author's perspectives and craft.
- Ability to address all elements of a higher-order interpretive question about a text.

Source: Adapted from a reading rubric formerly part of the Arizona State Assessment Program, Arizona Department of Education, Phoenix.

Student Responsibility and Behavior

Student responsibility and behavior are an integral part of growth and development; they dramatically affect the academic climate of a school (Blase 1986, McPherson 1972, Lickona 1991).

James Fitzpatrick is a former principal and superintendent. While he was principal at Champlain Valley High School in Burlington, Vermont, he instituted a set of innovative disciplinary practices. He believed that the burden for order and responsibility should be on students, including giving them more of a part in determining the rules they would live by and the consequences of their misbehavior. In the first year he implemented his system, the cost for repairs from vandalism dropped from $12,000 to $1,200. Suspensions were re-duced from 90 to 9. For the six following years, the school did not have to suspend any children. Because the intent of this new ap-proach was to re-engage, rather than to punish students, the dropout rate fell from about 7.5 percent to between 0.5 percent and 2.7 percent

FIGURE 7.6

Level 4 Criteria for a 4-Point Rubric for Responsibility

- Student demonstrates self-regulation by setting and following through on goals and by regularly monitoring and reflecting on behavior.
- Student is resourceful and knows how to seek assistance when necessary.
- Student is dependable and meets obligations and deadlines.

Source: Nash Elementary School, Tucson, Arizona.

annually *over the next seven years.* The new system dealt so effectively with students in a conventional school setting that one of the two alternative schools was closed.

At Tucson's Keeling Elementary, the number of violent incidents during one school year was reduced from 99 to 4 when the school implemented a new policy on campus fights. The school had no doubts about the policy's effectiveness.

La Cima Middle School instituted a new responsibility plan that produced significant results. From June 1992 to June 1994, the number of incidents in the category of "campus/classroom disruptions" was reduced from 588 to 402. The number of unexcused absences and tardies, as well as incidents of vandalism, theft, and arson, was halved.

As many schools are demonstrating, the concept of responsibility can embrace a larger set of behaviors. Figure 7.6 shows part of a 4-point responsibility rubric used at Nash Elementary School in Tucson. The rubric also includes descriptions of nondisruptive behavior (not included in the figure). Data on students, class, and school performance on this rubric are collected and charted regularly—even weekly in some classes. A 2nd grade teacher at Nash pointed out how effective it is for him to chart his class's behavioral performance daily and weekly. He likes to encourage his class by saying, "Look at this. We had a great day yesterday. Most of us are at '4'—what are we going to do today? Let's do it again."

Such imaginative use of a responsibility rubric has had measurable dividends for the teacher and the school. It creates clear, understandable goals and subgoals for students and staff.

"Unconventional" and Affective Measures

Throughout this book, I have stressed the primary importance of academic goals and lamented the perennial avoidance of striving for clear learning and behavior targets that we can measure progress toward. We are wise to remember what Joyce, Wolf, and Calhoun (1993) tell us: They "did not find a single case in the literature where student learning increased but had not been a central goal" (p. 19).

Academic goals, however, do not preclude using other kinds of targets and measures. We can expand the idea of results to include measures of processes that are a step or two removed from actual student achievement or behavior. When coupled with a vigilant attendance to achievement or behavior, such measures can bring about positive change. Except in rare cases, the following targets should not be a substitute for the school's annual improvement goals; they do not deserve as much time or attention. They would usually be subordinate to learning goals.

"Unconventional measures," a term Peters (1987, pp. 491–492) uses, can be among the most significant and effective ways to foster change where it counts. Speaking in the context of business, he advocates that we embrace and elevate the status of some common-place activities by gauging and displaying the number or percentage of each:

- People or teams involved in "small starts" (improvement efforts).
- Rewards given for quality.
- Pilot projects.
- Ideas swiped from competitors.
- People working in teams.
- Recognition acts or events per month.
- Time spent per day or week on a top priority.
- Hours and dollars devoted to upgrading skills.

Many of these activities will translate to school settings. Similarly, schools may measure and chart progress toward other goals:

- Training (e.g., the number of teachers confidently employing more engaging, interactive, and constructivist learning techniques).
- Number of team-based improvement efforts.
- Number of goal and data-driven improvement efforts.
- Number of good ideas disseminated and adapted.

Or what about measures that help us adjust processes to move toward the goal of increasing the number of students who complete assignments? The root causes for why students don't turn work in—not just homework but all assignments—may reveal ways we can incrementally enhance the quality and capacity of school work to arrest their energies. The 9th grade "Freshman Forum" program at

Amphitheater's Canyon Del Oro High School found a strong correlation between student failure and failure to turn work in. On the basis of this information, the Forum teachers brainstormed for strategies to help ensure that more students would complete and turn in assignments. The results of their preliminary efforts were at least modestly encouraging.

The issue of work completed brings us to a cornerstone issue—and another ripe opportunity. Both Goodlad in the 1970s and Lounsbury and Clark as recently as 1990 have given us the grim news: For a vast majority of students, school is too often a series of passive and often boring activities. Haberman (1990) tells us that the most disadvantaged and disaffected students are being fed a diet of meaningless drill and worksheets, even though such methods were "never proven by research or practice." Numerous studies, including those by Newmann (1992), and by Means, Chelemer, and Knapp (1991), point out what common sense should have already told us: Students don't learn much from dull, meaningless exercises and assignments. This situation may be one of the root causes for student disaffection, especially in secondary school where it is most pronounced.

One way to measure progress in this area is to document how schools are becoming more challenging, enjoyable, and engaging places to learn. At Hollibrook Elementary School, teachers ask students directly about their level of satisfaction with their experience there. As many as 90 percent have indicated that they enjoy school and like their teachers.

A consortium of schools called the North Carolina Project have attempted to invigorate science instruction by introducing a more active, hands-on curriculum. Part of what the schools wanted to accomplish in the short term was a new attitude toward science. They succeeded—in spades. After only one year of implementation, the percentage of consortium students reporting that they like science rose from 38 to 87 percent (O'Neil 1992).

Social Behavior and Character Development

One category on the 1st grade report card in the Ann Arbor Public Schools is "Learning and Social Behaviors." Included with the academic indicators are items that measure behavior:

- Demonstrates self-control.
- Follows directions.
- Completes tasks independently.
- Respects the rights of others.

In any school, the data in such areas can provide a rewarding context for collaboration. For example, if the data indicated a persistent problem in following directions, teachers can discuss democratic procedures that heighten student buy-in and understanding of classroom rules. The data would regularly reveal progress and areas most needing intervention.

One of the most creatively data-driven school districts I have visited is the Clovis, California, schools, which have an exceptionally strong tradition of promoting measurable growth in the areas of "Mind, Body, and Spirit." The Clovis schools developed imaginative ways to promote and measure "Spirit" and character development long before it was fashionable. Teachers systematically gather data on student involvement in volunteer activities, which they believe are tantamount to character development. At some schools, students acquire points for a variety of activities:

- Maintaining a flower bed on campus.
- Helping clean up after a dance.
- Visiting a nursing home.
- Participating in extracurricular activities (which correlates closely with students staying in school).

Students accumulate points to earn an award recognizing their accomplishment. Principal Richard Sparks of Valley Oak Elementary School in Clovis spoke enthusiastically about the increasing number of students who have earned the "Exemplary Wildcat Award" over the years. These results are discussed regularly, as teachers develop new strategies for reaching out to more and more kids who benefit from the experiences these programs offer. These, too, are meaningful results.

The Challenge

The challenge, especially in the beginning, is to be supremely protective of the number of goals we pursue formally—the goals for which we establish regular times for analyzing data and planning for improvement. These other goals, though important, do not—should not—supplant the central academic goals of a school. They are meaningful subgoals and ancillary goals, but the frequent and regular time and attention needed to reach learning and behavioral goals must take precedence. As we have seen so many times, schools can make progress toward affective and procedural goals and still not make any substantive progress in student learning. This tension is resolved by being ever watchful of the results that represent a school's primary academic and behavioral mission.

Taking Advantage of Available Data

Even before we have the chance to develop and refine more sophisticated assessments and ways of measuring progress, we would be smart to capitalize on the many opportunities we have to begin gathering meaningful data immediately. In Frederick County Public Schools, school improvement teams set goals and then make use of whatever data are appropriate—and available. Steve Hess, their director of assessment, shared how this approach can include the most available and easily assembled data:

- Number or percentage of students on the honor roll, per quarter.
- Number or percentage of students receiving an *A* or *B* in subject areas that are the focus of the year's goals.
- Decrease in number or percentage of students receiving *D* or *F* in specified subjects.
- Number of students completing algebra or geometry.
- Reduction in the number of students moving out of the lowest quartile.
- Schoolwide or grade-level GPA.

Common End-of-Course Assessments

Common end-of-course assessments also represent a readily available opportunity for data-driven improvement and curricular coherence. For Michael Fullan (personal communication, 1999), assessment is the "coherence-maker" in school improvement efforts. As we have seen in places like Stevenson High School in Lincolnshire, Illinois; the Pomperaug School District in Connecticut; Frederick County Public Schools in Maryland; Glendale Union High School District in Arizona; and, more recently, the Lake Havasu, Arizona, Schools, common end-of-course assessments can exert a profound influence on what is taught and talked about.

Initially, teams of teachers can create these assessments from existing final exams—actually saving teachers time while improving the quality of assessments. With time, teachers can modify the assessments to conform to changes in state or district standards. The creation and ongoing refinement of such assessments is one of the most concrete and powerful professional development experiences teachers can have.

Bank the Best

It can take an exceedingly long time to acquire first-rate assessments for all the areas mentioned in this chapter. Therefore, we must bank, borrow, share, and organize the best assessments and assessment tools to make them available to every teacher in our schools, states, and districts. Pomperaug and Frederick County schools, as well as the Maryland State Assessment Consortium, have made a science of pooling their best assessments. Their teachers can choose from a wealth of fine assessments and evaluation criteria that are refined yearly. Frederick County teachers believe they saved years by working to develop high-quality assessments with 16 other districts. These assessments can be purchased and adapted by any interested district.

So what are we waiting for? From the conventional to the more sophisticated, we have opportunities in every area to begin gauging—and getting—improved results.

Conclusion: Leadership

If I had enough ribbon, I could conquer the world.

—Napoleon Bonaparte

Change throughout the system will not come about through a thousand points of light, but from the steadily increasing, concentrated light and heat of one sun.

—Donahoe 1993

Celebrate, Recognize, Reinforce, and Reward

The kind of significant, sustained improvement that we need in schools will not occur in an isolated, free-lance culture, where no one knows what anyone else is doing or what each other's operative goals are. That is a system in disarray.

Schools improve when purpose and effort unite. One key is leadership that recognizes its most vital function: to keep everyone's eyes on the prize of improved student learning. The crush of competing agendas and distractions does not make that focus easy.

One of the most effective means to cultivate a goal-oriented culture is to regularly reinforce and recognize improvement efforts, both privately and publicly. The business world is beginning to realize the importance of such recognition, which brings an organization closer to its goals (Peters 1987). But not schools. Lortie (1975) found that schools were conspicuously lacking a sense of pride or achievement, that individual as well as group recognition of progress or success was extremely rare. More recent research by Evans (1993) indicates that "in most schools, recognition levels are chronically low," at a time when the challenges of change make such recognition and reinforcement more important than ever (p. 22).

We are failing to take advantage of what students in both business and industry tell us may be the most potent and effective aspect of leadership, with the best chance of promoting change and improvement (Peters 1987, Blase and Kirby 1992). Little (1987) asserts that for teachers to work effectively together, "the accomplishments of individuals and groups must be recognized and celebrated" (p. 514). Sincere, regular praise, plus recognition and celebration of accomplishment, may be the most overlooked ingredient in results-oriented leadership. Blase and Kirby (1992) found that praise from administration was the most frequently cited source of good feelings, and that most teachers have unfulfilled needs for recognition and approval. Lortie's (1975) observations indicate that this need has a direct impact on a school's ability to get results:

> [The] modesty of occasions which produce prideful feelings underscores the difficulty teachers see in attaining worthwhile results (p. 133).

He found that teachers "crave reassurance which, for them, could only come from superordinates or teaching peers." The absence of this reassurance not only "reduces the joy" of teaching but also leads many teachers to seek professional fulfillment by concentrating only on their strong suits—and giving short shrift to subject areas or students who make them feel less successful (Lortie 1975, p. 141).

Teachers can guide themselves in many meaningful ways, but principals and other leaders have a responsibility to reinforce individual and collective effort. The school community can help by taking the time to establish common goals that direct not just individuals but all faculty members in a socially interactive, mutually reinforcing effort. Establishing goals is a manifestation of leadership, but it is only the beginning in a results-oriented framework. Just as regular consultation of data and indicators is essential to sustained, targeted effort, so also is regular praise, recognition, and celebration necessary to keep the effort focused and energized. Success and improvement are every bit as social as they are structural. An atmosphere of acknowledgment and appreciation is essential.

Administrators at every level can be more effective if they use concrete strategies to celebrate and recognize goal-oriented effort and achievement. Praise and public acknowledgment that "yes, you or your team really do make a difference" is both confirming and affirming in a culture that has traditionally been marked by a high level of "uncertainty" about the significance of its contributions (Lortie 1975, pp. 134–136). Attempts to more regularly and publicly appreciate quality efforts can make a difference—more than perhaps any other factor (Blase and Kirby 1992, Peters 1987).

Goals, Data, and Leadership: A Reciprocal Relationship

Again, the first step is to establish goals. Goals and data make achievement clear and intelligible, hence easier for a busy leader to recognize. In Frederick County, Maryland, schools have given year-end dinners for members of school improvement teams to publicly celebrate the goals achieved at each site. In Amphitheater schools, former Superintendent Richard Wilson asked teams of teachers to give presentations to school and district administrators, describing their data-driven success in reaching their goals. Efforts like these provide a public forum for praise, while providing explicit and inspiring examples of what an organization most values.

Initial improvement efforts are not always sustained. We have seen how improvement ceases when a gifted leader moves on. Leadership should lead to results; if we wish to see a new generation of leaders who can truly lead us to better results, then we must adjust the system to facilitate such leadership.

The new culture of schools should encourage and expect that a leader will orchestrate a program that includes measurable goals, as well as regular praise and celebration of progress toward those goals. "Leadership" should "demand short-term results" and thus "spread hope" (Chang, Labovitz, and Rosansky 1992, pp. 101–102). Our graduate schools and leadership academies should teach such leadership. Without a set of common goals, schools will not be able to sustain their efforts, hope will dwindle, and low expectations may set in. With it, the entire school community can work as one. Collaboration will not happen, however, if goals are too numerous, superficial, or unmeasurable.

Leadership must unite. In her studies, Little (1990) remarks on the gross, unsettling inconsistency in activities and emphases she observed among teachers all supposedly teaching the same subject—English. Managing a "thousand points of light" is feckless and probably impossible. But we don't have to advocate a rigid, lockstep uniformity for leaders to effectively manage a coherent, unified effort to help more kids learn to write, read, and use mathematical knowledge.

Celebration, recognition, and reward only require a varied repertoire of methods and a sincere heart. Teachers must believe that the methods are more than a bald attempt to manipulate or control behavior. They must see praise and recognition as an extension of a leader's character (Blase and Kirby 1992).

Praise must also be tied to specific successes, even targeted to both individual and group accomplishments. The result, as teachers themselves attest, is a more focused, creative, positive, and supportive faculty. To bring this about, leaders can use some of the following methods:

- Leaving notes in boxes or on a desk, complimenting effective instruction that was observed.
- Giving coffee mugs for individual or group achievements.
- Offering a trinket or gift (a big favorite in one workplace was candy bars).
- Briefly, but frequently, praising, celebrating, and recognizing efforts at faculty meetings or board meetings.
- Prominently featuring graphs and charts—similar to the United Way thermometer—where employees can regularly view their progress and school leaders can easily refer to goal-oriented progress.
- Providing opportunities for successful teams to share their accomplishments in brief presentations at administrative meetings. Perhaps every major meeting should begin with such presentations.
- Providing opportunities for individuals to share a goal-oriented success with other groups or school faculties.
- Ensuring that every issue of the school or district newsletter highlights team and individual accomplishments; some issues could contain banner headlines, with charts and graphs revealing growth.

To promote faculty involvement in reward and recognition, leaders can use a "Recognition Nomination Form" like the one at the end of this chapter (see p. 118).

"Field" of Dreams, Where Progress and Recognition Prevail

Many teachers work in near anonymity, regardless of their daily and weekly accomplishments. They deserve recognition; our schools can only benefit from granting it. When deserving people are not appropriately appreciated for all they do, entropy may rush in. In her book, *Leadership and the New Science*, Margaret Wheatley (1994) likens organizational life to what physicists call a field, which consists of particles. Fields—bad or good—form as "particles" converge to create a palpable reality. "Vision," morale, and the spirit of an organization are a function of the particles that create a field—prevailing and evolving thoughts and conversations that occur in thousands of situations (pp. 47–56).

Unfortunately, the spirit of many organizations, regardless of their written vision statements or beliefs, reveals a lack of critical density. Into this vacuum can rush rumor, mistrust, and negativism. The organization becomes aimless—a mass of "contradicting fields... a jumble of behaviors," with no clear purpose (Wheatley 1994, pp. 56–57).

Leaders, then, must be what Wheatley calls broadcasters, targeting praise and recognition to create a unified, purposeful culture or field. Developing a positive, productive, and fulfilling field in a school or district means providing contexts and flashpoints that promote positive and productive thoughts and conversations. If we frequently clarify and celebrate progress toward goals and the impact of our efforts on students, we help to sustain the conditions essential to a healthy, ever-improving workplace. Just as important are efforts to recognize, reward, and celebrate accomplishments, which work preemptively to ward off the destructive thoughts and conversations that are the inevitable result when an organization ignores the social and psychological needs of its people.

Leaders must facilitate this. They must bring the field into being—and broadcast confidence in what the organization can achieve. Thoreau tells us to advance confidently toward our dreams, even to build "castles in the air....That is where they should be. Now put the foundations under them" (Thoreau 1946, p. 21). Management theorist Russel Ackoff (1978) encourages leaders to lead participants in a discussion of the perfect organization and the loftiest goals—to construct an "idealized redesign" based on their loftiest aspirations (p. 189). Then the group can brainstorm for practical ways to realize the dream. He describes his concept:

> An idealized redesign of a system reveals that the principal obstructions between an organization and what it most wants to be lie within the organization, and that these barriers can be removed (p. 190).

Leaders are uniquely positioned to ensure that amid the busyness and bombardment that all organizations endure, the dream remains central. Leaders nourish the dream by keeping each person fully aware of an organization's purpose and goals. Individuals also need to know that, without a doubt, their efforts contribute meaningfully to the purpose and goals. By providing brief but regular occasions to observe, recognize, celebrate, and reward meaningful accomplishments, leaders can create a field of dreams where progress and appreciation prevail.

Central Office Leadership

As Chapter 2 emphasizes, school administrators must break their own unfortunate habit of avoiding specific, improvement-focused collaboration. Their dialogue—about technical, logistical, or attitudinal problems we will inevitably encounter despite the best planning—must be regular and frank. To slight this is to presume that administrators are quite capable of dealing with problems by themselves; that most of them won't have any serious problems, anyway; or that there isn't enough time for such dialogue. None of these objections makes any sense in a learning organization.

The primary responsibility for ensuring effective, ongoing, problem-focused dialogue falls to the district leadership. District leaders must initiate this dialogue and develop guidelines for making it productive. Even 30 to 60 minutes a month of focused dialogue about anonymously submitted problems or challenges could begin to generate hope and practical solutions to the inevitable—and potentially crippling—problems encountered on the road to improvement.

Similarly, it is the responsibility of district administration to coordinate the optimal use of funding and time—including summertime and intersession breaks—toward continuous learning and improvement. With the help of school staff, they must ensure that staff development, follow-up, school improvement planning, and the effective use of early release times are not left to chance, but are strategically planned to promote better results. The absence of such deliberate planning in these areas is one of the most alarming realities of education in our time.

The Importance of Teacher Leaders

Because school administrators occupy a unique position in school organizations, we have been stressing their importance as "broadcasters," as keepers of the focus. Nonetheless, the most interesting lesson we have learned in the past few years is that leadership—especially at the school level—almost has to include teacher leadership. It is the rare principal, however intelligent or committed, who can take a faculty and single-handedly communicate, create, and realize the vision of higher achievement.

The reasons are not mysterious. On the one hand, principals play a central, symbolic role in schools. They typically evaluate teachers and carry the weight of responsibility for the school's performance. This rightly entitles good building administrators to a certain deference and respect.

But principals do not, at the ground level, have to implement instructional changes themselves. Teachers are vividly aware of this. Change has a much better chance of going forward when principals team up with teachers who help to translate and negotiate new practices with the faculty. The combination of principals and teacher leaders is a potent combination, as so many schools demonstrate.

It is high time we formalize such leadership in the following ways:

1. Designate—and cultivate—talented teacher leaders at every school. Ideally, they should be both competent and respected members of the faculty. Department heads or the equivalent should be chosen on this basis—rather than on seniority or popularity.

2. Pay them a reasonable stipend. Leadership is not free. Teacher leaders should be given at least a modest stipend. Hour for hour, their compensation should certainly be no less than what we pay coaches.

3. Provide them with release time. Find ways to relieve them with substitute teachers or by finding creative ways to give them a few hours whenever possible. Even modest amounts of regularly scheduled time can go a long way.

4. Include them in administrative training. Teacher leaders become a principal's most valued ally and interpreter of effective structures and methods.

5. Involve the faculty in their selection. Invite teachers and administrtors at the district level to establish results-oriented criteria and expectations for these positions. Then on the basis of the criteria, ask school faculties to help select the teacher leaders, perhaps for a designated term.

These processes themselves can become an opportunity to emphasize the centrality of student learning and improvement.

Ultimately—haven't we all seen this?—leadership can be exercised by any staff members who assume responsibility for their school or district's success, who attempt to favorably influence even one other member of the organization. In ways formal and informal, everyone has opportunities to lead.

Is there a need for better, stronger instructional leadership from principals? Absolutely. But paradoxically, it could be argued that the strength of an organization inheres in its capacity for broad-based, participative leadership (Lambert 1998) and that we must be careful not to become overly dependent on the principal to move forward (Fullan and Donahoe, cited in DuFour and Eaker 1998, p. 182).

Schools might develop a form like the following "Recognition Nomination Form" (see p. 118). This form clearly lays out the criteria for targeted, results-oriented recognition and celebration. A school or district recognition committee might meet periodically to weigh nominations against the criteria as they select employees to be honored at staff meetings or other occasions.

Collective Brainpower—The Key to Results

This book attempts to influence the field that is our current school culture—in both what it does and how it thinks. The thoughts expressed here are offered with the confidence that the teachers, administrators, schools, and scholars mentioned in these pages demonstrate the power of these enduring principles. They rescue us from mere "reforms," from "initiatives," to issue in what Glickman calls "solid, enduring results" for our children. Together, these principles point up the importance of taking full and systematic advantage of the greatest yet most underestimated resource we have at our disposal in the service of results: individual and collective intelligence. When we harness and organize this intelligence, improvement occurs. But if we want the stuff of dreams—sustained improvement on a wide, even national scale—only leadership will get us there. All of us, from community members to teachers to administrators, are in a position to influence the field on which the battle for better schools is taking place.

Recognition Nomination Form

Nominations should focus on extra effort made toward reaching school goals. For example:

- Exercising leadership focused on measurable results
- Maintaining a constructive, positive attitude toward reaching school learning goals
- Helping to develop common, periodic assessments
- Implementing and sharing research or new teaching ideas that promote better results
- Gathering or organizing data and evidence of improvement
- Helping to ensure that meetings are efficient and effective—that they result in great teaching ideas that get improved results for students

I nominate _____ for outstanding effort in helping our school to reach its measurable student learning goals.

This person has helped us to make progress toward our school goals by:

_____

_____

_____

_____

_____

Appendix:
Effective,
Time-Efficient
Meetings

The following model enables a team to have a productive meeting in about 30 minutes (which is often all that is available).[1] It can be tailored to fit a group's specific purposes. The approximate number of minutes for each part is in parentheses.

Before the Meeting
- **Agenda.** Was the agenda distributed in advance of the meeting? Is it posted in clear view of the participants?
- **Recording Tools.** Is flip chart, chalkboard, or computer ready to record brainstorming?
- **Designated Tasks.** Have the timekeeper, recorder, and facilitator been appointed?

During the Meeting
The team leader should establish and articulate the purpose of the meeting: What outcomes are desired? (The general purpose proposed for these meetings is to identify major concerns and strategies to promote better results for an agreed-upon goal.)*(1 minute)*

---

[1]The model was designed by Rosemary Beck, Bill Bendt, and Chris Potter, teachers in the Amphitheater School District, Tucson, Arizona.

Strategies That Worked *(5 minutes)*

What worked? The team leader gives each member a chance to offer evidence of a strategy that was effective in helping reach the goal since the last meeting.[2]

Chief Challenges *(3–5 minutes)*

What is the most urgent concern, problem, or obstacle to progress and better results?

Proposed Solutions *(8–10 minutes)*

What are possible concrete, practical solutions to these problems?

Action Plan *(10 minutes)*

- Which solutions might be best for the team to focus on between now and the next meeting? For example, if the goal or subgoal is "to increase the number of quality introductions," the team might focus on a strategy such as, "students will analyze model introductions before attempting to revise their own." (If agreement does not emerge quickly, rank-order voting to determine the focus may be useful.)
- If appropriate, the team may need to determine and record the names of the people who are responsible for specific tasks prior to the next meeting.

After the Meeting

The team leader distributes a memo documenting the team's focus between now and the next meeting. (A memo may not be necessary if brainstorming is done on a computer or using an LCD [liquid crystal display]; memos can then be printed out and distributed almost immediately.)

Summary

The meetings enable every team member to quickly and efficiently take advantage of the maximum number of concrete ideas and each member's acquired expertise on a clear goal and strategic focus.

---

[2]The emphasis should be on *concision*. You may want to limit the time for each brainstorming contribution by applying what Allied Signal Corporation calls the "20-second rule." This method not only increases the amount of ideas that each member generates but also heightens energy level, focus, and clarity of expression.

References

Ackerman, D.B. (1989). "Intellectual and Practical Criteria for Successful Curriculum Integration." In *Interdisciplinary Curriculum: Design and Implementation*, edited by H.H. Jacobs. Alexandria, Va.: Association for Supervision and Curriculum Development.

Ackoff, R. (1978). *The Art of Problem Solving*. New York: Wiley.

Adler, M. (1982). *The Paideia Proposal*. New York: Collier.

Andrade, J., and H. Ryley. (November 1992). "A Quality Approach to Writing Assessment." *Educational Leadership* 50, 3: 22–23.

Antil, L.R., J.R. Jenkins, S.K. Wayne, and P.F. Vadasy. (Fall 1998). "Cooperative Learning: Prevalence, Conceptualizations and the Relation Between Research and Practice." *American Educational Research Association Journal* 35, 3: 419–454.

Arizona Daily Star. (July 21, 1994). "Inner City School Pesters, Prods Pupils onto College," p. A1.

Association for Supervision and Curriculum Development. (1994). *Understanding the Conflict over Outcome-Based Education* (audiotape). Alexandria, Va.: Author.

Astuto, T.A., D.L. Clark, A. Read, K. McGree, L. de Koven, and P. Fernandez. (1994). *Roots of Reform: Challenging the Assumptions That Control Change in Education*. Bloomington: Phi Delta Kappa.

Atwell, N. (1987). *In the Middle: Writing, Reading, and Learning with Adolescents*. Portsmouth, N.H.: Boynton/Cook.

Bamburg, J., and E. Medina. (1993). "Analyzing Student Achievement: Using Standardized Tests as the First Step." In *Assessment: How Do We Know What They Know?* edited by J. Bamburg. Dubuque: Kendall-Hunt.

Berliner, D., and U. Casanova. (1993). *Putting Research to Work in Your School*. New York: Scholastic.

Berrueta-Clement, J.R. (1984). *Changed Lives*. Ypsilanti, Mich.: High Scope.

Bishop, J.H. (June 1995). "Improving Education: How Large Are the Benefits?" Written testimony delivered before a U.S. Senate Subcommittee on September 2, 1995. *Network News and Views*: 21–37.

Blase, J.L. (1986). "A Qualitative Analysis of Teacher Stress: Consequences for Performance." *American Educational Research Journal* 23: 13–40.

Blase, J., and P.C. Kirby. (December 1992). "The Power of Praise—A Strategy for Effective Principals." *NASSP Bulletin* 76, 548: 69–77.

Brigham, S.E. (1994). "TQM: Lessons We Can Learn from Industry." Anthologized in *Quality Goes to School*. Arlington, Va.: American Association of School Administrators.

Brooks, J.G., and M.G. Brooks. (1993). *In Search of Understanding: The Case for Constructivist Classrooms*. Alexandria, Va.: Association for Supervision and Curriculum Development.

Bullard, P., and B.O. Taylor. (1993). *Making School Reform Happen*. New York: Allyn and Bacon.

Byham, W.C. (1992). *Zapp! in Education*. New York: Fawcett Columbine.

Caine, R.N., and G. Caine. (1991). *Making Connections: Teaching and the Human Brain*. Alexandria, Va.: Association for Supervision and Curriculum Development.

Carbo, M. (1986). *Teaching Students to Read Through Their Individual Learning Styles.* Englewood Cliffs, N.J.: Prentice-Hall.

Carnine, D. (December 8, 1993). "Facts Over Fads." *Education Week* 13, 14: 40.

Cawelti, G. (1995). *Handbook of Research on Improving Student Achievement.* Arlington, Va.: Educational Research Service.

Champion, R. (Fall 1998). "'Sort of' Is Not Getting Us There." *Journal of Staff Development* 19, 4: 7.

Chang, Y.S., G. Labovitz, and V. Rosansky. (1992). *Making Quality Work: A Leadership Guide for the Results-Driven Manager.* Essex Junction, Vt.: Omneo.

Clark, D., S. Lotto, and T. Astuto. (1984). "Effective Schools and School Improvement: A Comparative Analysis of Two Lines of Inquiry." *Educational Administration Quarterly* 20, 3: 41–68.

Clarridge, P.B., and E.M. Whitaker. (October 1994). "Implementing a New Elementary Progress Report." *Educational Leadership* 52, 2: 7–9.

Cookson, P.W. (1985). *Preparing for Power: America's Elite Boarding Schools.* New York: Basic Books.

Cox, J. (April 8, 1994). "Meet This Year's Quality Cup Winners." *USA Today,* p. 3B.

Criscuola, M. (Fall 1998). "Achieving the Summit." *Journal of Staff Development* 19, 4: 14.

Csikszentmihalyi, M. (1990). *Flow: The Psychology of Optimal Experience.* New York: Harper Perennial.

Daggett, W. (June 1994). "Today's Students, Yesterday's Schooling." *The Executive Educator* 16, 6: 18–21.

Daniel, L. (1993). "Aligning Curriculum, Instruction and Assessment for a K–12 Writing Program." In *Assessment: How Do We Know What They Know?* edited by J. Bamburg. Dubuque: Kendall/Hunt.

Darling-Hammond, L. (November 1998). "Using Standards to Support Student Success." *Restructuring Brief* #15: 3.

Darling-Hammond, L., and A.L. Goodwin. (1993). "Progress Toward Professionalism in Teaching." From *Challenges and Achievements of American Education* (The 1993 ASCD Yearbook), edited by G. Cawelti. Alexandria, Va.: Association for Supervision and Curriculum Development.

David, J. (May 1994). "School-Based Decision-Making: Kentucky's Test of Decentralized Decision Making." *Phi Delta Kappan* 75, 9: 706–712.

Deming, W.E. (1986). *Out of the Crisis.* Cambridge: MIT Press.

Donahoe, T. (December 1993). "Finding the Way: Structure, Time, and Culture in School Improvement." *Phi Delta Kappan* 75, 4: 298–305.

DuFour, R. (April 1995). "Restructuring Is Not Enough." *Educational Leadership* 52, 7: 33–36.

DuFour, R., and R. Eaker. (1998). *Professional Learning Communities at Work: Best Practices for Enhancing Student Achievement.* Bloomington, Ind.: National Educational Service.

Edmonds, R. (October 1979). "Effective Schools for the Urban Poor." *Educational Leadership* 37, 1: 15–24.

Educators in Connecticut's Pomperaug Regional School District 15. (1996). *A Teacher's Guide to Performance-Based Learning and Assessment.* Alexandria, Va.: Association for Supervision and Curriculum Development.

ERS Bulletin. (December 1990). "Biology Education," p. 4.

Evans, K.M., and J.A. King. (March 1994). "Research on OBE: What We Know and Don't Know." *Educational Leadership* 51, 6: 12.

Evans, R. (May 1989). "The Faculty in Midcareer: Implications for School Improvement." *Educational Leadership* 46, 8: 10–15.

Evans, R. (September 1993). "The Human Face of Reform." *Educational Leadership* 51, 1: 19–23.

Fiske, E.B. (1992). *Smart Schools, Smart Kids: Why Do Some Schools Work?* New York: Touchstone.

Folzenlogen, P. Speaker at *Fortune Magazine* Education Summit, Washington, D.C., Sept. 23, 1993.

Frankl, V.E. (1963). *Man's Search for Meaning: An Introduction to Logotherapy.* New York: Pocket Books.

Fullan, M. (1993). "Innovation, Reform and Restructuring Strategies." In *Challenges and Achievements of American Education* (The 1993 ASCD Yearbook), edited by G. Cawelti. Alexandria, Va.: Association for Supervision and Curriculum Development.

Fullan, M. (1994). "Teacher Leadership: A Failure To Conceptualize." In *Teachers as Leaders: Perspectives on the Professional Development of Teachers,* edited by D. Walling. Bloomington: Phi Delta Kappa.

Fullan, M., and A. Hargreaves. (1996). *What's Worth Fighting for in Your School?* New York: Teachers College Press.

Fullan, M.G., and M.B. Miles. (June 1992). "Getting Reform Right. What Works and What Doesn't?" *Phi Delta Kappan* 73, 10: 745–752.

Fullan, M.G., with S. Stiegelbauer. (1991). *The New Meaning of Educational Change.* New York: Teacher's College Press.

Gamoran, A., and M. Nystrand. (1992). "Taking Students Seriously." In *Student Engagement and Achievement in American Secondary Schools,* edited by F.M. Newmann. New York: Teachers College Press.

Gardner, H., and V. Boix-Mansilla. (February 1994)."Teaching for Understanding—Within and Across the Disciplines." *Educational Leadership* 51, 5: 14–18.

Gitlin, A. (Summer 1990)."Understanding Teaching Dialogically." *Teachers College Record* 91, 4: 537–563.

Glickman, C.D. (May 1991). "Pretending Not to Know What We Know." *Educational Leadership* 48, 8: 4–10.

Glickman, C.D. (1993). *Renewing America's Schools: A Guide for School-Based Action.* San Francisco: Jossey-Bass.

Goodlad, J.I. (November 1975). "Schools Can Make a Difference." *Educational Leadership* 33, 2: 108–117.

Goodlad, J.I. (1984). *A Place Called School.* New York: McGraw-Hill.

Goodlad, J.I. , M.F. Klein, and Associates. (1970). *Behind the Classroom Door.* Worthington, Ohio: Charles A. Jones.

Greene, B., and S. Uroff. (February 1989). "Apollo High School: Achievement Through Self-Esteem." *Educational Leadership* 46, 2: 80–81.

Guskey, T.R. (March 1994). "What You Assess May Not Be What You Get." *Educational Leadership* 51, 6: 51–54.

Guthrie, J.W. (March 1993). "Do America's Schools Need a 'Dow Jones Index'?" *Phi Delta Kappan* 74, 7: 523.

Haberman, M. (December 1990). "The Pedagogy of Poverty Versus Good Teaching." *Phi Delta Kappan* 73, 4: 290–294.

Haladyna, T.M., S.B. Nolen, and N. Haas. (June–July 1991). "Raising Standardized Achievement Test Scores and the Origins of Test Score Pollution." *Educational Researcher* 20, 5: 2–7.

Hartmann, J.A., E.K. DeCicco, and G. Griffin. (November 1994). "Urban Students Thrive as Independent Researchers." *Educational Leadership* 52, 3: 46–47.

Hillocks, G., Jr. (May 1987). "Synthesis of Research on Teaching Writing." *Educational Leadership* 44, 8: 71–82.

Hodges, H. (March 1987). "I Know They Can Learn Because I've Taught Them." *Educational Leadership* 44, 6: 3.

Hopfenberg, W.S., H. Levin, G. Meister, and J. Roers. (1990). "Accelerated Schools." Accelerated Schools Project paper, Stanford University.

Hopkins, D. (1993). *A Teacher's Guide to Classroom Research.* Buckingham: Open University Press.

Hopkins, D., and M. West. (1994). "Teacher Development and School Improvement: An Account of the Improving the Quality of Education for All (IQEA) Project." In *Teachers as Leaders: Perspectives on the Professional Development of Teachers*, edited by D. Walling. Bloomington: Phi Delta Kappa.

Howe, H., II, and M. Vickers. (July 14, 1993). "Standards and Diversity Down Under." *Education Week* 12, 39: 36.

Jaeger, R.M., B.E. Gorney, and R.L. Johnson. (October 1994). "The *Other* Kind of Report Card: When Schools Are Graded." *Educational Leadership* 52, 2: 42–45.

Jones, R. (April 1995). "Writing Wrongs." *The Executive Educator* 17, 4: 18–24.

Joyce, B., M. Weil, and B. Showers. (1992). *Models of Teaching.* New York: Allyn and Bacon.

Joyce, B., J. Wolf, and E. Calhoun. (1993). *The Self-Renewing School.* Alexandria, Va.: Association for Supervision and Curriculum Development.

Katzenbach, J.R., and D.K. Smith. (1993). *The Wisdom of Teams.* New York: Harper Business.

Kohn, A. (September 1993). "Turning Learning into a Business: Concerns About Total Quality." *Educational Leadership* 51, 1: 58–61.

Krashen, S. (1993). *The Power of Reading.* Englewood, Colo.: Libraries Unlimited.

Lambert, L. (1998). *Building Leadership Capacity in Schools.* Alexandria, Va: Association for Supervision and Curriculum Development.

Lickona, T. (1991). *Educating for Character.* New York: Bantam.

Lipsitz, J., and R.D. Felner, eds. (March 1997). "A *Kappan* Special Insert on Middle Grades Research." *Phi Delta Kappan* 78, 7: 517–556.

Little, J.W. (1987). "Teachers as Colleagues." In *Educator's Handbook*, edited by V. Richardson-Koehler. White Plains: Longman.

Little, J.W. (Summer 1990). "The Persistence of Privacy: Autonomy and Initiative in Teachers' Professional Relations." *Teachers College Record* 91, 4: 509–536.

Livingston, C., S. Castle, and J. Nations. (April 1989). "Testing and Curriculum Reform: One School's Experience." *Educational Leadership* 46, 7: 23–25.

Lortie, D.C. (1975). *Schoolteacher: A Sociological Study.* Chicago: University of Chicago Press.

Lounsbury, J.H., and D.C. Clark. (1990). *Inside Grade Eight: From Apathy to Excitement.* Reston, Va.: National Association of Secondary School Principals.

Lowe, J. (1998). *Jack Welch Speaks.* New York: Wiley.

Maeroff, G.I. (March 1993). "Building Teams to Rebuild Schools." *Phi Delta Kappan* 74, 7: 512–519.

Maeroff, G.I. (1994). "On Matters of Body and Mind: Overcoming Disincentives to a Teaching Career." In *Teachers as Leaders: Perspectives on the Professional Development of Teachers,* edited by D. Walling. Bloomington: Phi Delta Kappa.

Malen, B., R.T. Ogawa, and J. Kranz. (February 1990). "Site-Based Management: Unfulfilled Promises." *School Administrator* 47, 2: 30–59.

Marzano, R.J., and S. Arthur. (1977). "Teacher Comments on Student Essays: It Doesn't Matter What You Say." University of Colorado, Denver: ERIC ED 147864.

Marzano, R.J., and J. Kendall. (1996). *A Comprehensive Guide to Designing Standards-Based Districts, Schools and Classrooms.* Alexandria, Va.: Association for Supervision and Curriculum Development.

Marzano, R.J., and J.S. Marzano. (1988). *A Cluster Approach to Elementary Vocabulary Instruction.* Newark, Del.: International Reading Association.

Marzano, R.J., D. Pickering, and J. McTighe. (1993). *Assessing Student Outcomes.* Alexandria, Va.: Association for Supervision and Curriculum Development.

McDonald, J.P. (1993). "Planning Backwards from Exhibitions." In *Graduation by Exhibition: Assessing Genuine Achievement,* by J. McDonald, E. Barton, S. Smith, D. Turner, and M. Finney. Alexandria, Va.: Association for Supervision and Curriculum Development.

McGonagill, G. (1992). "Overcoming Barriers to Educational Restructuring: A Call for 'System Literacy.'" ERIC, ED 357512.

McPherson, G.H. (1972). *Small Town Teacher.* Cambridge: Harvard University Press.

Means, B., C. Chelemer, and M.S. Knapp, eds. (1991). *Teaching Advanced Skills to At-Risk Students.* San Francisco: Jossey-Bass.

Mortimore, P., and P. Sammons. (September 1987). "New Evidence on Effective Elementary Schools." *Educational Leadership* 45, 1: 4–8.

Muncey, D., and P.J. McQuillan. (February 1993). "Preliminary Findings from a 5-Year Study of the Coalition of Essential Schools." *Phi Delta Kappan* 74, 6: 486–489.

Murphy, J.A. (October 1988). "Improving the Achievement of Minority Students." *Educational Leadership* 46, 2: 41–42.

Nadler, R. (June 1998). "Failing Grade." *National Review,* pp. 38–39.

National Council of Teachers of Mathematics (NCTM). (February 1994). *Algebra for Everyone* (a brief statement distributed to members). Reston, Va.: Author.

Newmann, F.M., ed. (1992). *Student Engagement and Achievement in American Secondary Schools.* New York: Teachers College Press.

New York State Education Department. (February 1998). *Assessment Bulletin.*

Noddings, N. (November 1997). "Thinking About Standards." *Phi Delta Kappan* 79, 3: 186–187.

November, A. (November 1998). "Creating a New Culture of Teaching and Learning." *Restructuring Brief* (No. 18). Santa Rosa, Calif.: North Coast Professional Development Consortium.

Odden, A., D. Monk, Y. Nakib, and L. Picus. (October 1995). "The Story of the Education Dollar: No Academy Awards and No Smoking Guns." *Phi Delta Kappan* 77, 2: 161–168.

Olson, L. (June 15, 1994a). "Writing Still Needs Work, Report Finds." *Education Week* 13, 38: 1.

Olson, L. (June 22, 1994b). "International Math and Science Study Finds U.S. Covers More in Less Depth." *Education Week* 13, 39: 10.

O'Neil, J. (September 1992). "Science Education: Schools Pushed to Broaden Access, Overhaul Practice." *ASCD Curriculum Update*: 1–5.

O'Neil, J. (March 1993). "Achievement of U.S. Students Debated." *ASCD Update* 35, 3: 1, 3–5.

O'Neil, J. (August 1994). "Making Assessment Meaningful." *ASCD Update* 36, 6: 1, 4–5.

Osborne, D., and T. Gaebler. (1992). *Reinventing Government: How the Entrepreneurial Spirit Is Transforming the Public Sector*. New York: Addison Wesley.

Palincsar, A.S., and L.J. Klenk. (1991). "Dialogues Promoting Reading Comprehension." In *Teaching Advanced Skills to At-Risk Students*, edited by B. Means, C. Chelemer, and M. Knapp. San Francisco: Jossey-Bass.

Parker, W.C. (1991). *Renewing the Social Studies Curriculum*. Alexandria, Va.: Association for Supervision and Curriculum Development.

Peters, T. (1987). *Thriving on Chaos*. New York: Alfred A. Knopf.

Peters, T., and R. Waterman. (1982). *In Search of Excellence*. New York: Harper and Row.

Peterson, D. (1991). *A Better Idea*. Boston: Houghton Mifflin.

Pikulski, J.H. (September 1994). "Preventing Reading Failure: A Review of Five Effective Programs." *The Reading Teacher* 48, 1: 17, 30–39.

Pogrow, S. (April 1988). "Teaching Thinking to At-Risk Elementary Students." *Educational Leadership* 45, 7: 79–85.

Pogrow, S. (February 1990). "A Socratic Approach to Using Computers with At-Risk Students." *Educational Leadership* 47, 5: 61–66.

Reich, R.B. (1992). *The Work of Nations*. New York: Vintage.

Resnick, L.B., V.L. Bill, S.B. Lesgold, and M.N. Leer. (1991). "Thinking in Arithmetic Class." In *Teaching Advanced Skills to At-Risk Students,* edited by B. Means, C. Chelemer, and M. Knapp. San Francisco: Jossey-Bass.

Richardson, J. (Fall 1998). "We're All Here to Learn." *Journal of Staff Development* 19, 4: 49–55.

Rosenholtz, S. (March 1989). "Workplace Conditions That Affect Teacher Quality and Commitment: Implications for Teacher Induction Programs." *The Elementary School Journal* 89, 4: 421–439.

Rosenholtz, S.J. (1991). *Teacher's Workplace: The Social Organization of Schools*. New York: Teachers College Press.

Rothman, R. (April 1, 1992a). "Science Reform Goals Elusive, NAEP Data Find." *Education Week* 11, 28: 15.

Rothman, R. (April 22, 1992b). "In a Pilot Study, Writing Is Gauged." *Education Week* 11, 31: 24.

Sarason, S.B. (1982). *The Culture of the School and the Problem of Change.* Boston: Allyn and Bacon.

Schaffer, R.C., and H. Thomson. (January–February 1992). "Successful Change Programs Begin with Results." *Harvard Business Review* 70, 1: 80–92.

Schaffer, R.H. (1988). *The Breakthrough Strategy: Using Short-Term Successes to Build the High-Performance Organization.* New York: Harper Business.

Schmoker, M., and R. Marzano. (March 1999). "Realizing the Promise of Standards-Based Education." *Educational Leadership* 56, 6: 17–21.

Schmoker, M.J., and R. Wilson. (1993). *Total Quality Education: Profiles of Schools That Demonstrate the Power of Deming's Management Principles.* Bloomington: Phi Delta Kappa.

Secretary's Commission on Achieving Necessary Skills (SCANS). (1992). *SCANS Report.* Washington, D.C.: U.S. Department of Labor.

Senge, P. (1990). *The Fifth Discipline: The Art and Practice of the Learning Organization.* New York: Doubleday.

Shanker, A. (April 4, 1994). American Federation of Teachers Advertisement. *The New Republic,* p. 43.

Shavelson, R.J., and G.P. Baxter. (May 1992). "What We've Learned About Assessing Hands-On Science." *Educational Leadership* 49, 8: 20–25.

Showers, B., B. Joyce, M. Scanlon, and C. Schnaubelt. (March 1998). "A Second Chance to Learn to Read." *Educational Leadership* 55, 6: 27–30.

Singham, M. (September 1998). "The Canary in the Mine: The Achievement Gap Between Black and White Students." *Phi Delta Kappan* 80, 1: 8–15.

Sizer, T.R. (1992). *Horace's School: Redesigning the American High School.* New York: Houghton Mifflin.

Slavin, R.E., N.A. Madden, L.J. Dolan, B.A. Wasik, S.M. Ross, and L.J. Smith. (April 1994). "Whenever and Wherever We Choose: The Replication of Success for All." *Phi Delta Kappan* 75, 8: 639–647.

Smith, M. (June–July 1991). "Put to the Test: The Effects of External Testing on Teachers." *Educational Researcher* 20, 5: 8–11.

Smith, P. (1985). *America Enters the World.* New York: McGraw-Hill.

Smith, P. (1987). *Redeeming the Time: A People's History of the 1920s and the New Deal.* New York: McGraw-Hill.

Smith, W.F., and R.L. Andrews. (1989). *Instructional Leadership: How Principals Make a Difference.* Alexandria, Va.: Association for Supervision and Curriculum Development.

Sparks, D. (Fall 1998a). "Making Assessment Part of Teacher Learning." *Journal of Staff Development* 19, 4: 33–35.

Sparks, D. (March/April 1998b). "Professional Development." *AEA Advocate,* pp. 18–21.

Sparks, D., and S. Hirsh. (1997). *A New Vision for Staff Development.* Alexandria, Va.: Association for Supervision and Curriculum Development.

Steele, C.M. (April 1992). "Race and Schooling of Black Americans." *Atlantic Monthly,* p. 75.

Stevenson, H. (September 16, 1998). "Guarding Teachers' Time." *Education Week,* p. 52.

Stiggins, R.J. (1994). *Student-Centered Classroom Assessment.* New York: Merrill.

Thoreau, H.D. (1946). *Walden, or Life in the Woods.* New York: Dodd, Mead.

Turner, D., and M. Finney. (1993). "The MultiMedia Exhibition." In *Graduation by Exhibition: Assessing Genuine Achievement,* by J. McDonald, S. Smith, D. Turner, M. Finney, and E. Barton. Alexandria, Va.: Association for Supervision and Curriculum Development.

U.S. Department of Education. (1998). "Policy Brief: What the Third International Mathematics and Science Study (TIMSS) Means for Systemic School Improvement." *Perspectives on Educational Policy Research.* Washington, D.C.: The National Institute on Educational Governance, Finance, Policymaking and Management; Office of Educational Research and Improvement.

Viadero, D. (February 9, 1994). "Impact of Reform Said to Be Spotty and Not Systemic." *Education Week* 13, 20: 1.

Walberg, H.J., G.D. Haertel, and S. Gerlach-Downie. (1994). *Assessment Reform: Challenges and Opportunities.* Bloomington: Phi Delta Kappa.

Walton, M. (1986). *The Deming Management Method.* New York: Perigee.

Walton, M. (1990). *Deming Management at Work.* New York: Perigee.

Waters, T., D. Burger, and S. Burger. (March 1995). "Moving up Before Moving on." *Educational Leadership* 52, 6: 35–40.

West, P. (April 1, 1992). "Math Teachers' Survey Finds a Schism Between Practice, Reformer's Vision." *Education Week* 11, 28: 1.

West, P. (December 8, 1994). "Efficacy of U.S. Aid for Science, Math Questioned." *Education Week* 14, 14: 1.

Wheatley, M. (1994). *Leadership and the New Science.* San Francisco: Berrett-Koehler.

Wiggins, G. (1993). *Standards, NOT Standardization.* Center on Learning, Assessment, and School Structure. Geneseo, N.Y.: Greater Insights Productions.

Wiggins, G. (July 1994a). "None of the Above." *The Executive Educator* 16, 7: 14–18.

Wiggins, G. (October 1994b). "Toward Better Report Cards." *Educational Leadership* 52, 2: 28–37.

Wolfe, P., and M. Sorgen. (1990). *Mind, Memory and Learning: Implications for the Classroom.* Fairfax, Va.: Patricia Wolfe and Marny Sorgen.

Index

Accelerated Reading Program, 13, 64–65
accountability, 4, 53–54, 87. *See also* assessment; data.
  new, results-oriented, 87
  professionalism and, 54–55
  sane and reasonable, 53
achievement
  connected to goals, 31
  research and, 73
Ackoff, Russel, 115
action research, 16–18, 26, 38
activity-centered programs, vs. results-driven programs, 66
Adlai E. Stevenson High School, Lincolnshire, Ill., 19
administration
  collaboration, 19–20
  leadership, 115–116
  recognition, 112
  training, 117
affective measures, 105–107
African American students, 57
aggregate analysis, 43–44
Algebra for Everyone (NCTM), 94
alignment of standards, instruction, and assessment, 74
alliances, teachers', 15
Allied Signal Corp., Tucson, Ariz., 48, 120
alternative assessment program, 97
American Federation of Teachers, 63
Amphitheater High School, 59, 81
Amphitheater Middle School, 57
Amphitheater School District, Tucson, Ariz., 18, 66, 99, 100, 101, 107, 113, 119
anchor papers, 83–84
Ann Arbor Public Schools, 103, 107
Apollo High School, Simi Valley, Calif., 50
artistic performance, 87
Assessing Student Outcomes (Marzano, Pickering, and McTighe), 92

assessment, 74, 89, 96–98. *See also* language arts; math; reading; science; social studies; writing.
  and accountability, 37, 42
  alternative. *See* Pomperaug Regional School District; rubrics.
  high stakes, 41
  performance, 50, 55
  of subject area content, 82, 89–95
  traditional, rubrics and, 85–87
Atwell, Nancie, 51
Australia, 91
autonomy, 41

Beck, Rosemary, 119
behavior, student, 104–105, 107–108
benchmark assessments, 97–98
Bendt, Bill, 119
Bessemer Elementary school, Pueblo, Colo., 57
Boothbay Harbor, Me., 51
brainstorming, 17, 18, 19, 46
breakthrough strategy, 56, 62
Brooks, Jacqueline and Martin, 38

Canyon Del Oro High School, Tucson, Ariz., 47, 107
Castner, Kevin, 4, 34
Centennial Elementary School, Evans, Colo., 28, 48, 66
central office. *See* administration; leadership.
Central Park East Secondary School, East Harlem, N.Y., 49–50, 96
challenge, 8, 108
Champion, Robby, 74–75
Champlain Valley High School, Burlington, Vt., 104–105
Champlin, John, 57
change, 7, 67–68

character development, 107–108
Cherry Creek Schools, Denver, Colo., 8
Chicago schools, 63
Christensen, Dolores, 99
Clovis, Calif., schools, 53–54, 108
Coalition of Essential Schools, 62, 86, 99, 101
collaboration, 12, 14. *See also* collegiality; teamwork.
 as action research, 16–18
 administrative, 19–20
 as key to improvement, 9–14
collective analysis, 43–44
collective assessment, 96–98
collective brainpower, 117–118
college, 8
collegiality, 10, 12
 effective, 15
 goals and, 25
 negative side, 15–16
 positive side, 16
Comer, James, 37
Common Assessment Tasks, 91
conservative bias, 12
Cookson, Peter, 101
cooperative learning, research on, 73
criteria, given to students, 60
criteria-based assessments, 37. *See also* rubrics.
Csikszentmihalyi, Mihalyi, 23, 42

Dade County, Fla., schools, 30
Darling-Hammond, Linda, 54
data
 abuses and excesses, 37
 available, 109
 dissemination and replication, 52–53
 failure to collect, 41
 fear of, 38–40
 and goals, 36
 group vs. conventional, 42–44
 "invisible," 44–46
 need for, 36–39
 performance, 44, 55
 periodic, 65
 reducing threat, 40–42
 results and, 42
 trends, 51
 used in specific school improvement ef-

forts, 36–52
 usefulness of, 44
data collection, 35, 41
 objections, 46–49
 successes, 49–52
data-driven school districts, 51, 108
dataphobic schools, 61
Deming, W. Edwards, 12–13, 27, 37, 46, 58
demystifying results, 78–84
Detroit Public Schools, Mich., 86, 103
development, research and, 74–75
direct instruction, research on, 73
disaggregating data, 60–61, 86
discipline, 104–105
discussion skills, 100–102
Dodge Park Elementary School, Prince George's County, Md., 25
Domino Sugar, 67
Donaldson Elementary School, Tucson, Ariz., 11, 46
dropout rates, going beyond, 77
DuFour, Richard, 19

economy, education and, 8
Edison, Thomas, 9
Edmonds, Ron, 38
education, 7–8
Educational Leadership, 6, 70
Effective Schools, 85
Elvira Elementary School, Tucson, Ariz., 86
end-of-course assessments, 109
Escalante, Jaime, 49
evidence, 53
excellence, disseminating examples of, 83–84
exemplary student work, 82–83
expectations, given to students, 60
experience, 2
expertise, 13, 17

Farmer, Noel, 22
fatalism, 39–40
fear of data and results, 39–40
feedback, 28
Fiske, Edward, 55
Fitzpatrick, James, 104
Flowing Wells District, Tucson, Ariz., 75
focus, 33, 45
follow-up. 17

Ford Motor Company, 11
format, 17–18
Fort Pitt Elementary School, Pittsburgh,
    Pa., 51, 57
Frankl, Victor, 24
Frederick County Public Schools, Frederick,
    Md., 4, 22, 34, 89, 109, 110, 113
free-lance culture, 26
Freshman Forum program, 106–107
frustration, 17
Fullan, Michael, 13, 38, 53, 109
funding and the school calendar (in rela-
    tion to professional development), 76,
    116
Gardner, Howard, 89
Garfield High School, Los Angeles, Calif.,
    49
General Electric, 62
Geneva City Schools, Geneva, N.Y., 75
George Westinghouse Vocational and Tech-
    nical School, Brooklyn, N.Y., 48, 57
Gilbert High School, Gilbert, Ariz., 99
Glendale Union High School District,
    Glendale, Ariz., 81, 109
Glickman, Carl, 28–29, 38
GM-Toyota NUMMI plant, Calif., 48
goal-averse culture, 26
goal-oriented culture, 111
goals, 22–34, 108, 113, 115. *See also* sub-
    goals.
        caveat, 32–33
        conditions for, 33–34
        criteria for, 31
        effective, 31
        interdependence with collaboration,
            purpose, and data, 9
        lack of, consequences, 23
        number of, 31–32
        psychological benefits, 64–65
        short-term, 63–64
        specificity of, 27–28
        student success and, 25
        teamwork and, 23–26
goal-setting and orientation
    at Centennial Elementary School, 28–
        29, 42
    concept, 55
    at Dodge Park Elementary School, 25
    at Frederick County schools, 22–23

at Mesa Verde Elementary School, 42, 45
    reducing threat, 40–42
Goodlad, John, 2, 27, 28, 23, 46

hands-on learning, 107
Havasupai Elementary School, Lake
    Havasu City, Ariz., 65
Hawthorne Elementary School, Seattle,
    Wash., 57
Hendery, Dan, 96
Hess, Steve, 89–90, 109
Hibbard, Michael, 97. *See also* Pomperaug
    Regional School District.
Higher-Order Thinking Skills (HOTS) pro-
    gram, 86
history, 58
Holaway Elementary School, Tucson, Ariz.,
    18, 96, 97
Hollibrook Elementary School, 107
hope, 20
*Horace's School: Redesigning the American
    High School* (Sizer), 97
Huberman, Michael, 12
humility, 20
Iacocca, Lee, 67
implementation, 28
improvement, 3, 5–9. *See also* assessment;
    data; goals.
        determining needs, 46
        incremental, 51–52
improvisation, incremental, 61
individualism, 10
initiatives du jour, 2
innovation, 2, 29, 30, 37
inquiry-based learning, 51
instruction, 73, 74. *See also* language arts;
    math; reading; science; social studies;
    writing.
instructional leadership, poor, 60
interdisciplinary learning, 89
isolation, 15, 27. *See also* collaboration;
    teamwork.
        breaking down, 44
        goals and, 25
        teachers, 9–11
Israel, 58

Johnson City High School, Johnson City,
    N.Y., 51, 65, 96

Johnson City School District, N.Y., 6, 51, 57

Joyce, Bruce, 38, 56, 73

Jump Start, 103

Junior Great Books (JGB) program, 86

Junior Great Books Foundation, 101

kaizen, 51

Kallick, Bena, 88

Katzenbach, Jon, 12–13

Kearney, A.T., 66

Keeling Elementary, Tucson, Ariz., 105

Kendall, John, 88

Key School, Indianapolis, Ind., 87, 99

Key School, New York City, 8

Kohn, Alfie, 36–37

Kyrene School District, Tempe, Ariz., 87, 98

La Cima Middle School, Tucson, Ariz., 48, 57, 105

Lake Havasu, Ariz., schools, 95, 109

Lake Wobegon effect, 78

language arts, 92–93

leaders, 115–117

leadership, 111–118

   central office, 115–116

   data and, 113–114

   recognition and, 114–115

   research and, 72

Leadership and the New Science (Wheatley), 114

learning, 20, 29. *See also* achievement; assessment; data; students.

   cooperative, research and, 73

leverage, 49, 62

Levin, Henry, 37, 38

listening, 16–17

literature, 92–93

Little, Judith, 12, 14

Littleton, Colo., schools, 41

Maeroff, Gene, 22

Maryland schools, 50–51, 83

Maryland State Assessment Consortium, 51, 110

Marzano, Bob, 88

math, 60, 65, 85–86, 93–94, 97

McTighe, Jay, 51

meetings

model for effective, time-efficient, 17–18, 119–120

   unproductive and ineffective, 14, 59

Mesa Verde Elementary school, 42, 45

Metropolitan Writing Exam, 57

Miles, Matthew, 38

momentum, 67–68

monitoring, 2, 5

multiplier effect, 9

multiple intelligences, reflected on report cards, 89

Nash Elementary School, Tucson, Ariz., 22, 105

National Assessment of Educational Progress report, 59

National Council of Teachers of Mathematics (NCTM), 93–94

National History Standards Project, 90

National Staff Development Council, 13

New York City schools, 4, 8

New York Regents Competency Exam in Mathematics, 65

New York Regents exam, 91, 96

North Carolina Project, 51, 57–58, 107

Northview Elementary School, Manhattan, Kan., 16

notebook surrogates, 94

Oak Harbor School District, Wash., 83

observations, firsthand, 53

optimism, 20

oral presentation, 99

outcome-based education (OBE), 6, 40, 41

overload, 32

Paideia Program, 101

Parker, Walter, 90

passive activities as boring and meaningless, 46, 107

patterns, data and, 43

pay-for-performance, 41

Peck Elementary School, Arvada, Colo., 14

performance data, concept, 55

Peters, Tom, 12, 48, 106

Peterson, Donald, 11

Phi Delta Kappan, 70

Pogrow, Stan, 86

politics, 1

Pomperaug Regional School District #15, Middlebury/Southbury, Conn., 50, 79, 91, 95, 96–97, 109, 110
potential for improvement, 61
Potter, Chris, 119
Poughkeepsie, N.Y., 8
poverty, children of, 60–61
praise. *See* recognition.
preparations, perpetual, 66–67
presentism, 10–11
Prince Elementary School, Tucson, Ariz., 13
principals, 112, 116
principles and practices, 1
private schools, 101
process, 4–5
productivity, 80
professional, "nonreading," 70
professional development, 74–76. *See also* leadership.
progress
   measurement, 39
   monitoring, 45
purpose, 80–81

quality work, 83. *See also* Total Quality Management.
quick wins, 62, 65–66, 68

rain dance, 66
Reading Recovery program, 58, 63, 102
Reading Renaissance, 102
reading, 8, 14, 58, 64–65, 102–104
   assessment of, 50–52, 72
   learning to read, 102–103
   reading to learn, 103–104
   research and, 72
   research-based approach, at Canyon Del Oro High School, 47
   and Success for All program, 47
reasoning-based methods, 85–86
recognition, 111–112, 113–115
Recognition Nomination Form, 117, 118
redesign, idealized, 115
re-engaging the student, 104–105
reform
   failure, 63
   goals and, 29–31
   rescue from, 118
Reinventing Government: How the En-

trepreneurial Spirit Is Tranforming the Public Sector (Osborne and Gaebler), 30–31
release time, 117
report cards, redesigning, 87–88
research, 70–74. *See also* data; results.
   on basic and higher-order skills, 71
   development and, 74–75
responsibility
   administration, 115–116
   student, 104–105
results, 3–4, 5, 6, 99–109
   among the disciplines, 99–108
   demystifying, 78–84
   examples of excellence and, 83–84
   key to, 117–118
   short-term, 5, 64–66, 69
results-driven programs, 63–64, 66
reward. *See* recognition.
Richmond County, Ga., middle school, 26
Rolewski, Mark, 22
rubrics, 37, 78–83, 84, 91
   examples, 92, 93, 97, 105
   as promoting learning and purpose, 80
   subject-area content, 82
   success from, 82–83
   traditional assessments and, 85–87

SCANS report (Secretary's Commission on Achieving Necessary Skills 1992), 100–101
science, 59–60, 87, 94–95
scoring guides. *See* rubrics
Senge, Peter, 6, 49, 70
Shanker, Al, 63
Sims, Nyana, 65
site-based management, 30, 31
Sizer, Ted, 97–98
skills, basic and higher-order, 71
Smith, Douglas, 12
social studies, 90–92
socioeconomic factors, research and, 61, 73
Sparks, Dennis, 13
Sparks, Richard, 108
spirit, 114
staff development, 74–76
   and time, 76, 116
   underfunded, 60
stakes, high, 41

Stand and Deliver, 49
standardized scores
  going beyond, 77–78
  norm-referenced, 84
standardized tests, 84–85, 86
standards, 74, 80, 98
Standards, NOT Standardization (Wiggins),
  80
statistics, 46–49
Stevenson High School, Lincolnshire, Ill.,
  109
Stiggins, Rick, 34, 39
Still, Suzanne, 38
stipends, 117
structure, 17–18
students
  achievement, 73
  engagement, lack of, 60
  evaluation, 43
  responsibility and behavior, 87, 104–
    105, 107–108
subgoals, 81, 102
subject area, 89–95
  content, assessing, 82
  knowledge, 82
success, 7, 20, 62
  measuring. *See* accountability; assess-
    ment; data; unconventional measures.
  short-term, 7
  stories, importance of, 41
Success for All program, 47, 102

tangibility, 44
targets, 33, 80
teachers
  collective brainpower of, 118
  collegiality of, 10–16, 25
  inadequate induction of, 60
  as leaders, 116–117
  poor, 40–41
teacher-to-teacher interactions, 15
team spirit, 41
teamwork, 9–21
  at Adlai E. Stevenson High School, 19
  at Amphitheater Schools, 18–19
  apparent, 15
  benefits, 11–14
  concept, 55
  at Donaldson Elementary School, 11

goals and, 23–26
informed, 2
at Northview Elementary School, 16
at Peck Elementary School, 14
problems, 15–16
results-oriented, 16, 18–19
at Thunderbolt Middle School, 13
at Wilkerson Middle School, 13
test scores, 78, 82. *See also* standardized
  tests.
Texas Scholars Program, 8
Thunderbolt Middle School, Lake Havasu,
  Ariz., 13, 14, 64–65
time, for school improvement efforts, 31–
  32, 76, 116, 119–120
Total Quality Management (TQM), 4, 28,
  30–31, 48, 64, 66, 68
  at Centennial Elementary School, 48, 68
  at George Westinghouse Vocational and
    Technical School, 48
  at Johnson City Schools, 6, 51, 57
  in industry, 5, 14, 48, 67
Toyota plant, Georgetown, Ky., 5, 14
Treisman, Philip, 57
Tucson Unified School District, 88
tutoring, 103

unconventional measures, 105–107
underperformance, 7
University of California at Berkeley, 57

Vallas, Paul, 63
Valley Oak Elementary School, Clovis,
  Calif., 108
variables, 46–47
vision, 114

Walbrook High School, Baltimore, Md.,
  99, 100
Walton, Mary, 27, 48, 64
Welch, Jack, 62
Weld County School District 6, Colo., 35,
  36, 83, 98
Wesley Elementary School, Houston, Tex.,
  73–74
Westwood School, Dalton, Ga., 85
Wheatley, Margaret, 114
Wiggins, Grant, 38, 51–52, 80, 87

Wilkerson Middle School, Birmingham, Ala., 13
Wilson, Richard, 66, 69, 113
win–loss records, 87
Wisdom of Teams, The (Katzenbach and Smith), 12
writing, 8, 11–12, 28, 57, 59, 65

assessment, 36, 46, 50–52
district assessment of, 87
research and, 46, 71–72
rubric/scoring guide, 79
Yunk, Dan, 16

zest, 66–67

About the Author

Mike Schmoker is a school improvement consultant living in Flagstaff, Arizona. As a central office administrator in two Arizona districts and a senior consultant for the Mid-Continent Regional Educational Laboratory (McREL) in Aurora, Colorado, Schmoker worked with teachers and administrators to promote and facilitate continuous improvement. He has studied and visited numerous schools and districts that demonstrate the effective use of continuous improvement principles. With Richard Wilson, he is coauthor of *Total Quality Education: Profiles of Schools That Demonstrate the Power of Deming's Management Principles,* published by Phi Delta Kappa.

You can reach him at 2734 N. Carefree Circle, Flagstaff, AZ 86004. Phone: 520-522-0006. Fax: 520-522-0007. E-mail: schmoker@future one.com.